KEYS OF THE KINGDOM

JESUS' DIVINE OBSESSION? DON'T MISS THE ONLY GOSPEL HE EVER PREACHED

By Rev. Dr. Ken R. Unger

Published by Transformation Media Incorporated
8211 San Angelo Drive, Suite J11
Huntington Beach, CA 92647

Manufactured in the United States of America.

ISBN: 978-1-961003-05-7

TABLE OF CONTENTS

PREFACE

JESUS HAD A DIVINE OBSESSION: **He was a man on a mission with a message.** Sadly, although I've studied the Bible almost every day for over five decades, I missed His major message and mission for most of my life. WOW! So glad I finally did the research. (Did you know that WOW is an acronym for Wonder Of Wonders?) Jeremiah 33:3 says if we call on the Lord, He will show us wondrous things that we know not of. *Keys of the Kingdom* is about those wondrous things.

You see, later in life, after I published comprehensive books on scriptural sexuality, discipleship, and end-time healing, I was plagued with a daunting question: why do most preachers and evangelists use heaven or hell to reach unsaved people when Jesus never did? My research stunned me! ***Jesus offered 'sinners' something far better than free fire insurance!***

I almost missed the best news that God offers us! Jesus came to give us the Keys of His Father's Kingdom!

As I sought to understand God's Kingdom better, I discovered that the topic is huge. Surely someone in church history wrote a comprehensive book on it! I searched and researched and not just on Amazon. I probed church history and famous authors who discussed

God's Kingdom, but my quest came up empty. ***Not one had written a comprehensive book on the most important topic in the entire Bible.***

Why do I call it that? As I dug deeper into the biblical essence of the Kingdom Gospel I got even more excited. Even if others had written a little about it, I felt compelled to tackle the entire topic. That meant breaking down almost half of Jesus's parables that He devoted to it. I also had to analyze all of the 150 times it's mentioned in the New Testament. Then I still had to consider the implications of the Promised Land in the Old Testament. As daunting as this task was, I couldn't ignore it. I was compelled to tackle it. Why?

Jesus said He won't return until the gospel of the Kingdom is proclaimed in every nation (Matthew 24:14)!

Here's why this is so essential. The Gospel of the Kingdom is hardly proclaimed in America and we send more missionaries to the world than anyone! I just had to research and write this book.

As I waded into this awesome and stimulating topic, I discovered something else. My 30+ years of global research on the horrific New World Order was totally relevant to this very topic.

What I'll tell you now sounds radical, like some crazy tin hat conspiracy theory, but it isn't. When I first stumbled on to this, it sounded radical to me too. Then a lady I never met visited the church I pastored and handed me a mini book. She said God told her to give it to me. I thanked her and never saw her again. A friend recently told me he thinks she was an 'angel unaware'. She may have been! As I read the mini book it confirmed and even expanded on the conspiracy research I had begun to do; research so terrifying I wanted to forget I even knew it. Here was more verified substance on the evil sinister satanic New World Order. I couldn't ignore it. It's like seeing something so horrific that you can never unsee it. Her mini book expanded way beyond what I learned and it had copious footnotes that corroborated everything. ***Our world contains far more evil than I ever imagined.***

I did all the research I could, even traveling to obscure libraries that had rare books I couldn't find elsewhere. Here's what I discovered: the globalist elite want to force a New World Order on us; one they can rule at the behest of Satan who, like Molech, Beelzebul and Baal in the Bible and other demonic pagan 'deities', demand to be appeased though child sacrifices! Furthermore, they want to depopulate 90% of the planet making it small enough for Satan to rule. Don't take my word for it, do your own research. Examine the UN's 2030 Agenda. Read the info from the Georgia Guidestone. With the internet today it's easy to see if I'm telling you the truth.

So what does Satan have to do with God's glorious Kingdom? ***Our loving God of the Bible has a radically different plan.*** People need not sacrifice their children to receive it. He sacrificed His Son so He could give it to us! And He didn't do that just so we could have pie-in-the-sky in the sweet by and by. ***He did it so He could give us the***

Keys of the Kingdom. And not just any kingdom. He made the supreme sacrifice to give us, you and me, the keys of the King of king's Kingdom! And He truly is omnipotent. He can rule the entire new heaven and new earth as His Word promises. There are 13 passages in the Bible that explain this. Just ask your cell phone to show them to you.

You see, He wants His people to rule over a New Heaven and a New Earth. I call it ***God's Great World Order.*** When Jesus preached the glorious good news of the Kingdom of God - ***the only gospel He ever proclaimed*** - He didn't just explain it through teaching and parables like most religious leaders do. His whole life showed us how we can make our world ***"on earth as it is in Heaven,"*** precisely as the Lord's prayer pleads.

Sadly, though millions of people hear sermons about Jesus every week, most preachers have also missed God's greatest good news. I pastored for 23 years and didn't grasp it either. What makes this really sad is that His real message, the complete scriptural gospel, is one for which everyone yearns; I know I sure did. I still do. It's so good I want more of it every day. ***Jesus' message and mission, His reason for coming to earth, is to proclaim and provide us with an abundant life (John 10:10).*** It's the very essence of that elusive thing He called blessedness or we might even call bliss. Sadly, many Christians seem to think that the abundant life Jesus came to give us is, well, almost a bad thing. One troubled fundamentalist preacher even wrote a book that says God doesn't want you happy! A pastor I know preached a whole series on it!

Who doesn't want to be happy? As I neared the end of

my senior year in college, that's all I wanted. As I faced the fear of going out into the real world, I turned down graduate scholarships to the best universities in the world, stepped off the academic merry-go-round and finally examined my life. I had achieved all my immediate goals. I was named 'Scholar of the Year', joined the best fraternity, had three marketable majors and a huge a resume of extracurricular achievements to make anyone proud. When a Fortune 500 executive saw my college resume he said it was the best he had ever seen. He hired me on the spot and paid me more then they ever paid a new hire. I also had a beautiful girlfriend, a bright future, and sadly, a gaping empty hole deep inside that I didn't know how to fill. Worse yet, I was plagued with a nagging fear that the path I was on might make me rich, but it would never show me the way to that elusive state we call happiness.

**The only thing I really wanted was happiness.
I just didn't know where to find it.**

Six months after graduation I finally discovered that ever elusive path to happiness, but not before almost destroying my health, my sanity and even my life. I found that hidden pathway in the last place I expected to find it - the Bible! And today, decades later, I'm still on that narrow joyful path which Jesus that so cryptically called the Way, the Truth and the Life.

The abundant life is an extraordinary lifelong journey.

His way is the highest of beautiful high roads but it can also plummet us to the deepest lows you will ever know. Ironically, the path to paradise sometimes leads through pain and privation, while it also lifts you to dizzying heights you can only imagine.

So why do I stay on that path? I can only tell you that once you embark on it, it ruins you for anything less. Deep down in your inner 'knower', you discover that there is no other Way to true happiness. So you somehow garner the courage to continue along His way. You realize you know too much to turn back now. To do so would be unfaithful to everything you are. Even during the darkest days, you have no choice but to proceed.

Many things tempted me to leave this path for easier roads – ones that crisscrossed less arduous routes and languished in more alluring neighborhoods. But in my heart of hearts, I knew that if I got off His Way it would only lead to a longer, harder, more arduous journey and ultimately, it would take me nowhere I truly want to go. Many shortcuts tempt us to avoid the daunting strenuous straight and narrow way. But I've learned that even the most pleasureful short cuts are deceptive dead ends. I've also learned that even your worst failures can propel you towards your greatest success.

Though it pales in comparison, I wrote this book to examine the major theme in the best book ever written. I designed it to help you understand things about the Greatest Good News ever shared. Some of its revelations expose blessings you could never imagine. Others will make you angry. They fly in the face of organized churchianity, both conservative and liberal. And that's how it should be. Biblical truth reveals nothing less than the delicious divine delectable mysteries of the Kingdom of Heaven. And such enigmatic trials should trouble us. I believe it was Mark Twain who said he wasn't bothered by the things in the Bible that he didn't understand, he was more disturbed by those he *did.* The Bible is an equal opportunity offender: there's something in it to bug everybody.

Most things are not what the majority thinks they are. Conventional wisdom is usually wrong and often quite foolish. Following the 'Narrow Path' of Jesus is very different from the broad one upon that the vast majority of people trod. It's harder but strangely also simpler. Mostly, it's far superior in every way to the wide road that leads to perdition in this life and the next. Both God's Book and this one point directly to He who alone is the Way. But it leads us to Him precisely because only He knows how to help us find the love, wholeness, joy, peace, fulfillment, purpose and yes, the ever elusive true health and happiness you crave. Thomas Kelly called these the "intimations of an astounding destiny." I just say WOW.

Good News Flash:
Jesus' message is as relevant to this life
as it is to the next.

Over 2,000 years ago, the One we call the Christ descended here to show us that ever exclusive experience called blessedness. The abundant life is at the core of His

Mission Statement (John 10:10). Isn't that also what the Beatitudes are all about? That beatific message, that inexplicably wonderful good news was and still is His divine obsession.

Why do I call it that? He spoke about God's Kingdom far more than anything else. It has little to do with judgmental admonishments about heaven and hell. John 3:16 is the most memorized verse in the Bible and also the most misunderstood. Most think it says *'For God so loved the world that He gave His only begotten Son so that whoever believes He exists shall not go to hell but go to heaven'.* Scripturally, saving faith requires us to so deeply believe in Him that we entrust our whole life to Him. Believing He existed is just a starting point, not what your eternal destiny is based on. Unless a person is born again he can't even see God's Kingdom let alone enter it (John 3:3). How do you know if you're born again? ***True disciples abide in Him*** (John 8:31)and those who obey Him will never even see death (John 8:51). ***Then there is John 3:17: Jesus didn't come into the world to condemn it but that through Him the world should be saved.*** He who was rich beyond comprehension willingly became poor so we could find the greatest treasure known to man (II Corinthians 8:9); a treasure so grandiose that we would joyfully sell all we have to possess it. Why? It pays enormous dividends in this life in addition to the most magnificent eternal retirement plan in the entire universe.

Jesus suffered the worst torment and the cruelest unjust death in history to help us find the only life worth living. It's a rich, full, blessed abundant life. And His joy in that,

His great reward? To create spiritual siblings out of the likes of you and me; to make us His brothers and sisters (Romans 8:29). ***For the joy set before Him, He endured the cross. That's how much we mean to Him!*** If we are wise enough to allow Him to transform us by making us Christ like, we will inherit with Him the greatest kingdom in the universe. Incredibly, we can become joint heirs with the King of all kings.

A beautiful hymn says *"A Love so amazing, so profound, truly deserves our very best."* To that end and for that purpose I share this book with you. My prayer and hope is that it can help to make your journey clearer and more focused; and that it compels you to find and comprehend the absolute Best News in the universe both for this life and the next. If you think you found the good news but it isn't all that great, this book will show you why and what you can do about it. If you've never found it, this book can help you even more. May you finally discover the fullness of His beautiful benevolent bliss.

NOTE 1: ***These are the keys OF the Kingdom, not TO it.*** There's a huge difference. If you have the key to a mansion, you can break into it. But if your father owns the mansion, he will teach you how you can possess it and never lose it. You must be an heir of the King of kings to receive such keys, for they reveal the sacred secrets you need to inherit the entire kingdom He wants to grant to you.

NOTE 2: I usually don't post scriptures in the text. But though this book shouldn't be controversial, it will be. So I'll post the most important scripture addresses in the text. That way you will know that it's not based on my thoughts, but on His all-powerful living Word.

NOTE 3: We will explore the seven major topics that comprise the Glorious Gospel of God's Kingdom. I'll then leave you an Addendum with key passages that even go beyond that. The more you explore the complete gospel of God's Heavenly Kingdom, the more blessings you find on earth. It's like a Kingdom great treasure hunt but better!

Yours in the Only Cause that truly matters,

Rev. Dr. Ken R. Unger

CHAPTER ONE

YOUR AWESOME INHERITANCE

Jesus said: "I must preach the good news of the kingdom of God to the other towns also, because that is why I was sent." - Luke 4:43

"I will give you the keys of the kingdom of heaven." - Matthew 16:9

"It is the Father's good pleasure to give you His kingdom." - Luke 12:32-4

YOU DON'T HAVE DIE TO ENJOY ETERNAL LIFE. That may sound strange because most of us were taught that the gospel concerns the next life. But Jesus' central message is a holistic and ever so practical gospel; one packed with extraordinary news for this life as well. It's the very best news in all of history. It isn't primarily about how to avoid bad news or even the worst news – Hell. The Bible wasn't written to just show us how to find the great news of pie in the sky when we die. Rather it is written to show us how to find fabulous news for this life as well; a veritable earthly foretaste of the next. It's steak on the plate while we wait! It's about an awesome way to live that carries over into the afterlife but certainly isn't limited to it.

The word gospel means good news, and the only good news that Jesus constantly shared with almost everyone to whom He talked was the splendid, extravagant, magnificent glorious good news of God's Kingdom. This message was the very essence of Jesus' divine obsession. It's central to the prayer He taught us: "Thy Kingdom come, Thy will be done, on earth as it is in heaven." His whole gospel is pertinent news that prepares us for heaven. And it's immediately available to whosoever wants it. Someone said everything you want in life comes through other people. This greatest news in the universe is no exception.

It's been rightly said that God's Kingdom is the Kingdom of right relationships.

This is the heart and soul of the life He labeled eternal. It's best defined as intimately knowing Abba Father God and Jesus Christ, the heavenly bride groom He sent to love and provide for us: His adoring bride (John 17:3). And make no mistake: knowing someone that intimately goes way beyond just having met him.

Many have said, Christianity isn't a religion, it's a relationship; One in which the indwelling Christ within us empowers us to develop healthy, genuine, intimate personal relationships with God and all others. When Jesus said "I am the Life", he was telling us that God's path is the pattern for true life, or at the very least a life well worth living. The emotional vibrational energy of God's Spirit animates all of life. That is the very nature of eternity invading this temporal earth through God's Only Begotten Son. He penetrates into the deepest heart of our life if only we are willing (John 1:12). Through the delicious, delectable, delightful Presence of the Holy Spirit in Jesus, Love paid a short visit to earth that totally transformed it forever. And He promises to stay with us whenever we welcome Him in. God who is love, fully incarnated the body of His only begotten Son. When we welcome Him to abide within us, He reincarnates Himself in and through us. That's the only human way to reincarnate, and it's much better than coming back as a sacred cow! It's only possible as we more fully yield to His beneficent Holy Spirit. That's the perfect way to experience the extravagant love, exuberant joy, and lavish abundance that accompanies our submission to Him as our heavenly husband.

Jesus knew that the astounding kingdom that God promises us contains everything any one could ever want and more. Better yet, as we'll soon see, Jesus knew that God's Kingdom is a very present reality through which any person can reap the benefits here and now, in this life. And it must be that way. The shop worn, religious, turn or burn 'gospel' of cheap fire insurance doesn't cut it. It's neither biblical nor wise. Who would work at a job without pay for their entire life just to get retirement benefits? Who believes they deserve hell if they don't accept it? I recently spilled scalding bacon greases on my thumb. It's the worst pain I ever felt on my skin. Should most people be tormented like that forever? As you'll see, that's not what God who is the very essence of love designed for any human.

No wonder Jesus was so passionate about God's Kingdom. Yet sadly, even today, we seldom hear much about His kingdom, and that's to our earthly and eternal detriment.

A quaint true story illustrates the point. A missionary landed in America after an arduous stint in Africa. As he deplaned, he noticed a huge crowd waiting to catch a glimpse of a famous rock star who had been seated in First Class. For a fleeting moment, the contrast between his own modest dress and nonexistent welcoming party and the rock star's bling, flashy clothes, fawning entourage and waiting limousine was too much to bear. *"Why doesn't anyone greet me like that, Lord?"* he silently pondered. *"Why do we suffer such deprivation on the mission field while this world's super stars get so much of everything when they get home?"* Then he heard God's still small voice within him whisper, "You're not home yet."

It's a lovely story, one that puts things into perpetual perspective. Or does it? As great as heaven is, eternal life is more than going to heaven when we die; much more. And many missionaries don't even know this. Jesus told us as much when he defined eternal life as personally knowing Him and God the Father (John 17:3). When we lose sight of that, we could forever lose the very people God wants most to touch and bless through us. We could lose our children, our friends, our neighbors, and perhaps even our own faith. The pie-in-the-sky-when-you-die mindset of most evangelism is woefully short lived. I'm told that Billy Graham's crusades reached out to millions of people but the retention rate of his converts hovered around a measly two percent. Most crusades seldom retain more than three percent of their 'converts'. I explain why this is an unbiblical and more importantly ineffectual and counterproductive methodology in my book, *PRECIOUS PEARLS*; a comprehensive scriptural tool for making disciples in any denomination. It even reaches agnostics and atheists.

Jesus and the Apostles never gave 'alter calls.' They never encouraged people to pray the sinner's prayer. Neither did Jesus. He didn't encourage decisions *FOR* Him, He made His followers disciples *OF* Christ. And He taught His disciples to do the same.

As an aside, Aimee Semple McPherson is the only woman to start a major denomination. It now has nine million members in 146 nations. She didn't believe in altar calls either. At her crusades she kept the altars open all night so people could 'tarry' there and seek God until they found Him. **She clearly understood that only those who are being led by the Spirit of God are the sons of God (Romans 8:14-17). Few people stay with Jesus if they don't experience His loving Spirit and the Bible doesn't make sense.**

Intellectual conversion isn't the Great Commission. Jesus commanded all His followers to make disciples in word and power (Cf. Matthew 28:18-20 and Mark 16:15-20). His great commission doesn't just apply to ministers and missionaries. They are mandated to equip all Christians to fulfill the great commission. This worked so well that Jesus' small handful of chosen followers reached the entire civilized world so effectively that in 400 years Christianity became the dominant belief system of the entire Roman Empire. It's still the largest organized religion in the entire world.

By Jesus' definition of eternal life, knowing the Lord means much more than just meeting Him. Many meet Him who never go on to truly know Him. Hence, they miss the amazing blessings promised to each of us when we *reincarnate* or embody His Kingdom realities in our own life. When someone told the great missionary David Livingstone how amazing it was that he had sacrificed everything to go to the mission field he said, "I gave up nothing of importance and gained everything of value. The mission field gave me back far more than I ever relinquished." As an aside, I'm told that he chose the name Living Stone to describe himself: a small stone compared to the huge rock of the apostle Peter.

Why do I say if we fail to learn this we could lose the people who mean the most to us? Consider this: a rapidly growing number of people are disenchanted with Christianity. According to the City University of New York's comprehensive American religious identification survey, the percentage of Americans who identify as Christians fell from 86 percent in 1990 to 77 percent in 2001. It's down around 60-65% today. This is in spite of the fact that the American Church spent a half trillion dollars on itself in the previous 15 years. That's a huge drop in a short period of time. The largest growing group in the survey was among those who don't subscribe to any religion. Their numbers more than doubled, from 14.3 million in 1990, when they constituted 8 percent of the population, to 29.4 million in 2001, when they made up 14 percent. I'm afraid to ask what it is today. I recently saw a teenager wearing a shirt that boasted about being a satanist!

This does not bode well for our society. Many of the problems we face as a culture, from drug use, corporate crimes, government corruption, divorce, and inner city blight, to social strife and conflict and an increasingly hostile attitude towards Christians, reflect these changes. Pollster George Barna's surveys showed that the majority of people see no difference between Christians and nonbelievers. If trends are not reversed, the quality of life in America will continue its steep decline and Christians here may soon suffer persecution no matter what they believe about the timing of the rapture.

Allegedly, 16 million people leave church each year never to return. During Covid, over 50% stopped attending. I've heard that a similar percentage of churches stopped meeting. Many stream their services now, and believe it's an adequate substitute. They don't realize that people watch the average online church service for just six minutes.

Why are people so eagerly abandoning church and Christianity? I'm not sure they are. I think they are fleeing from ***churchianity*** because they didn't see authentic Christianity there. Most churches probably haven't offered them the same faith Jesus offers us; a faith rooted in the great blessings and supernatural power of Kingdom Christianity. If they had, people wouldn't drop off so easily.

It bears repeating that Jesus said He came to give us - you and me - an abundant life (John 10:10). He promises us a greater love than any we have ever known (John 15:13-14); a love so exalted that it defies comprehension (I Corinthians 2:9). Along with that He offers us a delightful sense of joy that expands within us and endures forever (John 15:11). Who wouldn't want that? And what about peace? A 2011 survey found one in ten Americans are on antidepressants including 50% percent of pastor's wives (which is a very difficult job). Religion alone can't give anyone deep, true, everlasting shalom.

In addition to all those things, Jesus said He would give our lives significance (Mark 1:17). Rick Warren's book *The Purpose Driven Life* is one of the biggest best sellers of all time. In a generation hungry for meaning as well as happiness why would anyone not actively seek such blessings? When we see so many people walking away from their faith, perhaps it's because we Christians have been promoting the wrong product. When I say wrong, I mean a message very different from the one Jesus proclaimed.

Think with me for a moment about the purpose of the Bible. It's Literally a Testament; two testaments actually - an Old and a New one. But what exactly is a testament? The dictionary says it's a covenant between God and the human race. When capitalized it's either of two main divisions of the Bible. It's also an act by which a person determines the disposition of his or her property after death. The Bible is not called a last will and Testament, but that's what it is. It's a legal agreement between God and His people. It tells them the terms by which they receive an inheritance from Him. Years ago when I noticed how often the words heir and inheritance appear in the Bible I prayed to understand why. This next sentence is the answer and it's extremely important:

We don't receive an inheritance when we die, but when the one who gives it to us dies!

Let that sink in. The New Testament makes it very clear that God wants us to be His heirs (Galatians 4:7). He's adopted us (Galatians 4:5) and He wants to share with us an awesome inheritance (I Peter 1:4). ***That inheritance is nothing less than our Heavenly Father's Kingdom*** (Matthew 25:34). The whole Bible is packed with passages on heirs, joint heirs and inheritance.

A simple way to say this is that Jesus came to give us the keys of His Father's Kingdom (Matthew 16:19). He never proclaimed any other gospel. He had no other good news (Matthew 9:35). Easy-believism and cheap fire insurance just doesn't measure up. He said that God's Kingdom permeates our lives with divine power and blessings now, in this life, while we are yet living (Mark 9:1). It gives us power to change our world (Ephesians 3:20); power to make our fondest dreams come true (Psalm 37:4), and power to overcome any and all obstacles. Sadly, few of us know how to receive it let alone how to share it with others. Because of that we miss most of what God has for us. And if we don't even possess it, we can't pass it on to anyone else.

The Keys of God's Kingdom aren't just a way to open a door, they are the sacred secrets that provide you with everything beyond that door.

Turn or burn religion just doesn't do it for people any more. Perhaps it never did. In fact, it never should. To be sure, Jesus ***seems*** to speak more about hell than anyone in the Bible, however, the people He warned about hell as well as those He didn't, reveals so much about our God. He is the very essence of love and cherishes justice and righteousness. ***And the 54 verses translated hell in most English Bibles don't all mean what we think they do, as you'll see in the next chapter.***

This may surprise you: the only people Jesus warned about their impending damnation weren't terrible sinners or people who never heard about Him. They were the religious leaders who Jesus called white-washed sepulchers, broods of vipers and self-righteous religious hypocrites. Only one verse in the entire Bible refers to *Tartarus*, a literal hellacious damnation of the worst suffering possible in the "deepest abyss beneath the earth" (II Peter 2:4-6). It doesn't pertain to sinners who fall short of living gloriously, which is what sin means. It applies to the rebellious fallen angels who were cast out of heaven with Satan and also iniquitous people who willfully follow

Satan's ways. **Webster's Dictionary defines iniquity as "wickedness, gross injustice, corruption, debauchery, licentiousness and vice."**

What about the Lake of Fire? About 18 Bible passages discuss this. If you review them, you'll see that those who end up there are those who presumed upon God's grace and never even attempted to deal with the 39 moral absolute sins which invoke God's wrath and make them accursed. Included in that catalog are liars of all kinds and gossips.

When I researched this, I couldn't find one instance where Jesus threatened hell to any person we might consider to be an unlearned sinner. When a religious mob caught a woman in the act adultery and threatened to stone her to death (John 8:3), or He encountered a shady business man who no one liked (Luke 19:2), or a hated tax collector who ripped people off (Matthew 9:9-13) or a woman who had five husbands and was shacking up with yet another (John 4:18), Jesus didn't warn them about the next life, He offered them help with this one. His practical Christianity works wonderfully well. That's why within 400 years Christianity became the dominant force in the civilized world and it remains so today, encompassing well over two billion people around planet earth. It will work well for us also; much better than the steeply discounted partial gospel of eternal fire insurance that many religious people substitute for authentic scriptural discipleship.

That's why, to begin this study, we must revisit the Bible's teaching on hell. I must warn you, what you'll learn in the next chapter will shock you. But if you have ears to hear, it will open you up to a greater experience of God and the blessings that He wants for you than you have ever known possible. It will also redirect the Church to Jesus' methods of evangelism and change our entire world, just like it did between the first and fourth centuries. Follow along as we revisit the biblical doctrine of hell. It may shake your faith, but I promise this: I will establish everything I am about to share with you on a rock solid scriptural foundation. You can see for yourself if what I say is true. A simple web search will show you the four unique words translated hell in the English and where they are used in the Bible.

> *"The knowledge of the secrets of the kingdom of heaven has been given to you, but not to them." – Matthew 13:11.*

> *When will Jesus return: "And this gospel of the kingdom will be preached in the whole world as a testimony to all nations, and then the end will come" (Matthew 24:13-15).*

[NOTE: Jesus will return when His whole gospel is proclaimed to every nation.{

DISCUSSION QUESTIONS:

How does the Kingdom gospel differ from what you thought was the good news?

____

____

____

____

____

____

How do you feel now about the good news of God's Kingdom?

____

____

____

____

____

____

What if anything can keep you from embracing it?

____

____

____

____

____

____

CHAPTER TWO

THE BIBLICAL PROBLEM WITH 'HELL'

> *"And this is eternal life, that they would know You, the only true God, and Jesus Christ whom You have sent." John 17:3*

> *"For this is good and acceptable in the sight of God our Savior, who desires all men to be saved and to come to the knowledge of the truth." – I Timothy 2:3-4*

IN CRITIQUING THIS MISUNDERSTANDING OF HELL, a Christian author said this on the back of his book: ' "*God loves us. God offers us everlasting life by grace, freely, through no merit on our part; unless you do not respond the right way. Then God will torture you forever in hell." Huh?!*'

I love this blurb from Rob Bell's book *Love Wins*. It cuts right to the chase on a major issue that the vast majority of people in the world and thinking people in the church have with what they believe the Bible teaches. I haven't done studies on this and I suppose George Barna hasn't either but I'm pretty sure that most agnostics, atheists and nominal Christians are more perplexed angry and confused about the traditional doctrine of hell than anything else in church doctrine. And they have every right to be.

These flawed views of hell causes significant concern as many struggle to reconcile the God of love with the idea of eternal torment. This leads to a pervasive misunderstanding about both God's nature and humanity's ultimate fate. A turning point in understanding our faith may well revolve around how we define salvation. What does it mean to be saved? Is it merely a ticket out of hell, or is it an invitation into the fullness of life that Jesus promised?

Recent scholarship emphasizes that salvation is not just about avoiding punishment, it fundamentally concerns restoration and relationship. This means that the core of our faith calls us into a trans-formative journey; one that equips us to embody grace, compassion, and truth in a world that desperately needs hope. The early disciples totally understood this as they experienced the dynamic power of the Holy Spirit guiding them to heal the sick, liberate the oppressed, and proclaim freedom to the captives.

Today, the challenge remains the same. We stand at a crossroads where the Gospel must be presented in terms that resonate with those who feel disillusioned or disconnected. It requires us to reflect our understanding of 'good news' not simply in doctrinal terms but also lived and experienced in acts of love, commitment to justice, and expressions of authentic community.

Let us not forget that the early church thrived not

because of its right beliefs but because of its right actions, consistently demonstrating the transformational impact of God's Kingdom on every aspect of life. As modern believers we must ask if our churches embody the inclusive and active love of Christ, or are they perpetuating division and exclusion?

In light of this, we must reevaluate how we communicate our faith. We must emulate Christ's message of redemption instead of portraying shallow fear-based ultimatums. We must foster environments where people feel welcomed and empowered to participate in the divine narrative unfolding around them. Jesus's Kingdom gospel is as much about our present transformation as it is about our future hope.

DISCUSSION QUESTIONS:

How has your understanding of salvation changed over time?

____

____

____

____

____

____

____

____

____

What steps can we take to make our churches more inclusive and reflective of Christ's love?

____

____

____

____

____

In what ways can we actively participate in spreading a holistic gospel?

____

____

____

____

____

As we dive into the complexities of biblical doctrine, let this exploration of hell serve not only as an academic venture but as a personal journey toward a fuller understanding of God's heart for His creation. Remember, the goal isn't to fortify ideologies, but to dismantle misconceptions and build bridges that connect us back to the true and total grace that transforms lives.

It must make the Lord unspeakably sad to realize that most of the skeptics are right and most of us so called 'Bible believing' Christians are wrong. What if most of Jesus' greatest friends, with all their teaching, evangelism, bringing people to church and talking about God are actually making Him more enemies than converts? How repugnant is it to believe that God would send people to hell who never heard of Jesus or had a chance to receive His offer of eternal life? Is this compassionate Love? Is it merciful? Is it just?

What I'm about to share with you will seem controversial. By the time you read this, you may find that some knaves have twisted my words "to make a trap for fools," to coin Rudyard Kipling's brilliant poem "**IF**." I should warn you in advance: some people will misrepresent what I'm saying and accuse me of not believing in hell; some may even write me off as a heretic and say you should read no further. I expect that. As Albert Einstein once said, *"Great ideas always meet harsh resistance from mediocre minds."* I don't care about what kind of mind anyone has and I make no claim that these great ideas are mine; all I ask is an honest examination of the scriptures in the original language.

There is a literal hell, but most of what many of us have been taught about it is wrong and woefully misguided. Whether you like what I'm about to say or not, please know this about me: since I gave my life to the Lord in 1971, all I wanted was to follow Him closely. All I wanted then and now is to do whatever the Bible teaches. I've studied it almost every day since then and I daily continue to be astonished by what it says. It's the most fascinating and life-changing book in the world.

Here's the point I must make which some will find heretical: ***most of our modern Bibles use an unscriptural translation of the word we use for hell.*** All but one of the words erroneously translated as hell never referred to a place of eternal fiery retribution. This inaccuracy has harmed God's work on earth more than any other heresy in history. It's the ultimate doctrine of demons. No teaching does more to turn people off to the true Christian God of love, grace, mercy and compassion.

I find that most people chafe at the doctrine of hell as it's taught by either the Fundamentalist's or Universalist's. The latter group believes everyone will go to heaven. The former believes that only those who believe as they do will be saved. The accurate scriptural truth lies somewhere in between. And no solitary proof text is adequate to explain it literally and completely.

Even though I studied Greek and Hebrew in seminary, for years I didn't do my own examination of this crucial doctrine, preferring to use English translations and accepting them at face value. But I became increasingly uncomfortable with our evangelism methods. The question that launched me into this study was, ***"why do so many people use the hammer of hell and the promise of heaven for evangelism when Jesus never did?"*** After I carefully inspected what the Bible truly says about hell I was as shocked as you may be when you read what I'm about to tell you. You see, the word that is most often translated as hell in the Bible doesn't mean hell as we understand it today.

Consider these facts. In the King James Bible, hell is only mentioned 31 times in the Old Testament and 23 times in the New Testament. Of these 54 occurrences of the word hell, four different words have all been translated as hell in most English Bibles. By far, the one word used most is ***Sheol***. It's the only word for hell in the Old Testament, where it's mentioned 31 times. In the New Testament, ***Hades*** is the word *Sheol* and it's used for hell ten times, while ***Gehenna*** is used 12 times. ***Tartarus***, the one word that actually describes eternal fiery retribution, is used only once! Where did Peter find the word *Tartarus*? It was borrowed from ancient Greek mythology, not Judaism. ***The Jews had no concept of an eternal fiery hell. They didn't even have a word for an afterlife.***

Both *Sheol* and *Hades*, used 41 of those 54 times where hell is mentioned in the King James Bible, always meant *"the grave, the pit, or the abode of the dead"*. At best this means separation from God forever and while that isn't good, it's nowhere near as dreadful as being tortured by fire for all eternity. I can't stand that pain for a second when I accidentally pick up a hot dish, can you?

Again, the only word used for hell other than *Tartarus* that had any connection to fire is *Gehenna*. Jesus referred figuratively to *Gehenna* the huge garbage dump outside the city where trash burned all the time. As Rob Bell says, *"People tossed their garbage and waste in to this valley where a fire burned constantly to destroy the trash. Wild animals fought over scraps of food along the edges of the heap. When they fought, their teeth would make a gnashing sound. Gehenna was the place with a gnashing of teeth, where the fire never went out"* (*Love Wins*, p.68). **Except for *Tartarus*, none of the other words that were translated hell from the Greek or Aramaic and Hebrew refer to everlasting punishment in a fiery inferno.**

The solitary exception is where *Tartarus* is used in the Bible. It refers to a place of fiery eternal punishment for the fallen angels and people who followed Satan. (Read II Peter 2.) To be sure, the ungodly will be punished (verse 9), but that punishment is eternal destruction (II Peter 3:7), not Tartarus. The concept of an eternal fiery hell resembles doctrines from pagan demons and idols rather than the merciful, just, compassionate God of the Bible.

Both *Sheol* and *Hades* mean "the grave, the pit, or the abode of the dead". At best this means separation from the God for eternity and while that isn't good, it's nowhere near as bad as perpetually burning in unending torment for all eternity.

So where did we start substituting hell for *Hades* and *Sheol*? It appears to have begun with the Latin Vulgate from which the King James Version of the Bible was translated. Until the fourth century, the Apostles and earliest church fathers understood this. They taught that almost all people could eventually be saved; that God was so merciful He would eventually redeem just about everyone (Cf. I Peter 3:9). **The early church father named Origen even believed that Satan and his demons would eventually be saved!**

Most church fathers believed the Bible literally when it said Jesus was "the savior of all men, especially those who believe" (I Timothy 4:10). Wow, what a statement. When God said He was unwilling for any to perish but for all to receive eternal life, they felt He was fully capable of achieving that. But beginning in the fourth century, following the lead of a man most call Saint

Jerome, Augustine and Tertullian also began to teach the doctrine of "eternal hellfire". Apparently that was why Augustine went so far as to teach that unbaptized infants went to hell! This dreadful doctrine continued to be taught by Roman Catholics until recent years.

Jerome, who translated the Bible into Latin, used an incorrect translation of the word ***eon*** to indicate perpetual suffering forever. Kittel's definitive ten volume ***Theological Dictionary of the New Testament*** is the standard for biblical definitions. It says *eon* means 'Lifelong, and enduring'. This indicates a limited time, not forever. At the very least, as Rob Bell states, *"Eternal life is less about the kind of time that starts when we die, and more about equality and vitality of life lived now in connection to God. Eternal life doesn't start when we die; it starts now. It's not about a life that begins at death; it's about experiencing the kind of life now that can endure and survive even death"* (*Love Wins*, p. 59).

However Jerome, who was said to be a rather angry, antisocial, morose little man, apparently believed that the only way to make people obey God was to scare them into it. That may explain why he intentionally substituted the word hell for *Hades* and *Sheol* in his 'translation', stressing eternal damnation instead of the grave. He apparently felt it so necessary to terrorize people into obedience that he was willing to compromise his integrity as a translator.

The distinction between hell and *Sheol* is crucial. What if the fiery trials spoken of in the Bible -- a fire that consumes evil -- really refers to the baptism of fire of which Jesus spoke (Matthew 3:11)? What if this fire baptism is the purging and refining fire from God's Word and the tribulations of life that show people the consequence of disobedience, both in this life and the next? This was exactly what most ancient father's of our faith believed prior to Jerome's intentional mistranslations.

This earlier belief implies that Jesus truly is the Lamb of God who takes away the actual sins (not just the sin principle) of the world (John 1:29); that when God is unwilling that any should perish but that all should come to the knowledge of eternal life (II Peter 3:9), He can accomplish that. After all, *"Who can resist His will"* (Roman 9:19)? **If God wants all people to receive eternal life, why can't He pull that off?**

How would this work? Consider this: what if, on the other side of this life, there really is an opportunity for those who never heard the gospel to receive it? After all, this is probably why Jesus descended into *Sheol* after his death and before his resurrection: to offer eternal life to those held captive there (Romans 4:8-10); those who never had an opportunity to respond to Him. This is why, immediately after Jesus' death, people who had been long dead were seen walking through the streets of Jerusalem (Matthew 27:52-3). What if since then, on the other side of the grave, there's still an opportunity for salvation for those who need it when they face their life review. What if it's an opportunity when Jesus returns and every knee bows, for them to repent and follow Christ as Lord? This is totally consistent with thousands of highly credible near death experiences and it could explain the purpose of the millennial reign of Christ and the White Throne judgment (cf. Revelations 20). I personally know a number of non Christians who had near death experiences where they saw Jesus and were sent back to earth because He told them they had work to do. Much of that may mean working on themselves and sharing their message, and following Jesus wholeheartedly.

One verse commonly used to refute this possibility says we are all appointed to die once and then face judgment (Hebrews 9:27), but read it carefully. Nowhere does this passage say that these things happen immediately and that our fate is instantly and unalterably sealed. What if there is still one last opportunity for self examination, purging of sins and repentance? Wouldn't this be more consistent with a God of astounding love and mercy; one whose grace is sufficient for our every need? Wouldn't it better explain a God of true justice who also loves those who never heard of Christ. Or people who never saw it incarnated in a church where people were discipled to love God above all and their neighbors as themself? Isn't that possibly what Revelations 20 is all about?

Again, this was the position of the early church fathers until the fourth century. They believed that the baptism of fire (Matthew 3:11), something that virtually no one preaches about, would purge all people from their sins so they could accept Christ and follow him.

It makes perfect sense. If Jesus descended into Hades to preach deliverance to the captives who never had a chance to embrace his offer of eternal life, why wouldn't a just God give the same opportunity to others who never had a chance to know Jesus accurately in this life? If He didn't, could we call Him just? Would a righteous God sentence those to hell who never heard the good news along with those who rejected it? Could this explain why those who die without the law will be judged by the laws they believed (Romans 2:11-16)?

When the Bible is "rightly divided" (properly interpreted), we see that the doctrine of a fiery eternal hell was never a part of Jesus' Kingdom gospel, nor of the teaching of the apostles and the early church fathers. However, under the influence of Jerome's Latin Vulgate translation, the teaching of an eternal fiery hell was formalized in the Sixth Century by the Emperor Justinian who officially condemned the teaching of Universal Restoration – a doctrine that taught about the eventual potential salvation of all people.

You might say, wait, what about the scriptures that teach that a fiery hell awaits those who do not receive Christ? All such passages are found in symbolic teachings or metaphorical passages like Jesus' parables and the book of Revelations which is mostly a vision. Any responsible application of biblical hermeneutics (the science of biblical interpretation) teaches that metaphorical passages should not be taken literally. Fictional stories, poems, dreams and visions were never meant to be interpreted as factual depictions.

Whether you know it or not, you probably already apply that principle of hermeneutics. Consider this: Jesus freely used hyperbole - gross exaggeration - to make stunning theological points. If we believe that his injunction to pluck out our eyes or cut off our hands if they offend us must be taken literally (Mark 9:42-47), why doesn't anyone do that? We obviously don't act as if this were literally true. If we did, the Church would be full of crippled blind people!

I'm not saying there is no hell. As someone once said, *"The best argument for hell is Hitler, probably a Satanist, for whom it is just and necessary."* In fact, we are clearly told who will go to the end time lake of fire. That list is rather shocking: ***the cowardly, unbelieving, idolaters, and all liars will be sent there along with adulterers, sorcerers, immoral, murderers, and abominable (Revelations 21:7-8).*** Charles Simpson once said that the cowardly go into the lake of fire first because they wanted to do the things the really bad sinners did but they couldn't find the courage!

Of course, this indictment against gross sinners refers to unrepentant ones. Those who confess are forgiven for ***all unrighteousness*** (I John 1:9). This much grace causes some religious people serious problems. But that is precisely why Jesus told us that harlots will enter the kingdom before many religious 'leaders' (Matthew 21:31). His story of those who received a full wage for partial work further highlights this reality (Matthew 20:1-26). After all, grace is undeserved merit and favor. My favorite way to describe GRACE is God's Riches at Christ's Expense. Our good behavior can never pay for what Jesus bought for us. How good would you have to be to justify the sacrifice of God's only begotten Son?

The Bible clearly teaches that there is a literal hell and not everyone will go to heaven, but I believe we must revisit the commonly accepted doctrine of hell in light of solid biblical scholarship. We must also stop being so glib about hell. We must shelve the common fundamentalist position that threats of hell and promises of heaven are the best way to evangelize sinners. No doctrine has done more to turn people away from Jesus than an overly simplistic and unbiblical exposition of the doctrine of hell. I repeat: Jesus never ever used the hell hammer to club converts into the kingdom. Mohammed in the ***Qur'an*** mentions hell in one out of every 7.9 verses. But Muslims only *kill* people who refuse to convert in 09 verses in the Qur'an, according to Don Richardson. He listed all these passage on page 254 in ***SECRETS OF THE KORAN***. A simple web search also reveals them. Do we really believe that the biblical God who is the very essence of love is harsher than that and sentences them to eternal torment?

Some may say, "What about the Lake of fire?"

Surely we must consider that also. The results of this compilation are stunning to say the least, but read them very carefully:

> *Revelation 20:10 And the devil who deceived them was thrown into the lake of fire and brimstone, where the beast and the false prophet are also; and they will be tormented day and night forever and ever.*

Revelation 21:8 But for the cowardly and unbelieving and abominable and murderers and immoral persons and sorcerers and idolaters and all liars, their part will be in the lake that burns with fire and brimstone, which is the second death."

Revelation 20:15 And if anyone's name was not found written in the book of life, he was thrown into the lake of fire.

Revelation 19:20 And the beast was seized, and with him the false prophet who performed the signs in his presence, by which he deceived those who had received the mark of the beast and those who worshiped his image; these two were thrown alive into the lake of fire which burns with brimstone.

Matthew 18:8 "If your hand or your foot causes you to stumble, cut it off and throw it from you; it is better for you to enter life crippled or lame, than to have two hands or two feet and be cast into the eternal fire.

(Author's note: hyperbole anyone?)

Matthew 25:46 These will go away into eternal punishment, but the righteous into eternal life."

(Author's note: Read verses 40-46. Context is essential here.)

2 Thessalonians 1:8-9 ...dealing out retribution to those who do not know God and to those who do not obey the gospel of our Lord Jesus. These will pay the penalty of eternal destruction, away from the presence of the Lord and from the glory of His power,

Revelation 20:13-15 And the sea gave up the dead which were in it, and death and Hades gave up the dead which were in them; and they were judged, every one of them according to their deeds. Then death and Hades were thrown into the lake of fire. This is the second death, the lake of fire. And if anyone's name was not found written in the book of life, he was thrown into the lake of fire.

2 Peter 2:4 For if God did not spare angels when they sinned, but cast them into hell and committed them to pits of darkness, reserved for judgment.

(Again, please read the whole chapter for proper context.)

Matthew 25:41 "Then He will also say to those on His left, 'Depart from Me, accursed ones, into the eternal fire which has been prepared for the devil and his angels; ...

(As noted previously, verses 40-46 are essential.)

Please do your own research. I strongly suggest you read the whole chapter wherever you seek clarification.

An extra-biblical source I find intriguing are the three books of Enoch. They were widely read by early Christians and are in the canon in The Ethiopic and Slavonic Bibles. A friend had several near death experiences and took great comfort from his writings. She gave me an excellent translation by Joseph B. Lumpkin that explains ten heavens, not just three. It also explains fallen angels, the Nephilim and other topics I always wondered about.

Can you see why Jesus never used promises of heaven to persuade 'sinners' when he walked the earth. He knew people cared about this life before they gave thought to life after death. Unless a cynic is on their death bed, heaven probably won't be sufficient motivation for them to totally readjust their life. Today many people may work at a boring job their entire life in order to have security and a good retirement. But most won't follow a spiritual path that makes no sense to them just to get a great eternal benefit package and no tangible advantages until they die. Maybe we should try Jesus' approach. It's been said *if we want New Testament results we should try New Testament methods.* They certainly worked far better than what we've been doing lately.

Jesus offered us awesome good news: that we could become adopted as God's children (Ephesians 1:5), participate in the work of His Kingdom (Luke 9:60), enjoy its benefits in this life (Luke 8:1, 17:21), and ultimately even inherit God's Kingdom (Matthew 25:34).

The New Testament says we literally become His heirs; joint heirs with Jesus. And it's God's good pleasure to give us His Kingdom. That's good news that will preach to anyone. When you add to it the Kingdom's promises of righteousness, peace and joy in the Holy Spirit(Romans 14:17), who wouldn't want that? It's the Apostle Paul's definition of God's Kingdom. More on these marvelous kingdom benefits later.

Want More Stunning Good News?

I believe that a major reason why so few people evangelize is because most don't really believe that a loving and just God would send so many to hell and they mistakenly think that's what the gospel teaches. The hyper-fundamentalist teaching on hell doesn't square with the Lord they know and worship: a God of infinite love, compassion and mercy. He's a gracious, benevolent heavenly Father, not a judgmental hellacious dad: one who loves so lavishly that He sent His only begotten Son to die for us sinners. It also doesn't square with the Jesus they read about in the Bible who even forgave even those who crucified Him. It doesn't resemble a God who used someone like the murderous legalist Saul of Tarsus, who called himself the chief of sinners, to be His greatest messenger of eternal life and grace.

Hell is indescribably real, but I'm pretty sure it's reserved for Satan and his legions of demons, unrepentant sex traffickers who torture innocent infants for adrenachrome or sacrifice partial-birth abortion babies to sell their organs. Such evil people will be deservedly judged and condemned to everlasting punishment (Matthew 25:34, 42, 46, II Peter 2:4). But many fundamentalist Christians use an unscriptural doctrine of hell to scare people into a tepid half-hearted commitment to Jesus as Savior so they can go to heaven.

That doesn't working any more. Maybe it never did. Fewer young people identify as Christians than ever before; they call themselves, NONEs, as in their religion is 'none of the above'. Billy Graham always warned people about hell. I never heard an evangelistic sermon where he didn't. That's probably why 98% of those who came forward at his crusades fell away. This 'Graham Effect' evangelistic method seldom makes authentic decisions for Christ and with good reason: it's not how Jesus, Paul and the Apostles made disciples. It's a partial gospel, not the complete Gospel of the Kingdom.

The best way to reconcile the tension between the scriptures that refer to a fiery punishment with Universalism that promises ultimate salvation for all is to see it as one more enigmatic biblical paradox. It's similar to the tension between God's sovereignty and man's freedom. This approach to reasoning is challenging for westerners with a Greek mindset, but the Hebrews had no trouble with such paradoxes. Their middle eastern thought form is totally comfortable with the many seemingly irreconcilable differences that co-exist in scriptures. We in the west demand non-contradictory logic.

Those of us who have been educated in a Greek thought form can't stand contradiction. We demand that everything makes logical sense. But that's our problem, not God's. Like young children trying to comprehend quantum physics, we simply can't fathom certain deep mysteries of God. It's kinda like an ant trying to do algebra. How should we handle this? We're better off just saying, "God said it, I believe it, that settles it."

Some things will only become crystal clear when we are with our Lord in Heaven. Until then, we must accept many things in the Bible that only make sense when seen through the seemingly self contradictory lens of paradox. Perhaps for some, Hell is one of those things. But I know this: the Church will be far more effective if we proudly proclaim the only gospel Jesus stressed: His splendid preoccupation with God's awesome amazing Kingdom. That preaches much more profitably than any judgmental message of hellfire and damnation. Once this glorious complete good news is finally proclaimed to the entire world, and only then, will Jesus finally return (Matthew 24:14).

What exactly is Jesus' divine obsession?

Why is God's Kingdom mentioned 155 times in the New Testament while 'hell' is mentioned a scant 23 times? As we've seen, all but one of these are literally hellacious mistranslations. The glorious thing about God's Heavenly Kingdom is that it promises us everything anyone could ever want or need in this life as well as the next. It truly is what the world needs and craves now and at every time in history. It's what every generation longs for and always will. This is the kind of great 'good news' that anyone would be delighted to share with those we love. Join me as we explore the incredible Kingdom He yearns to give us (Luke 12:32). I guarantee it will change your life. It's continuously improving mine. Let's consider some relevant and very poignant scriptures:

"We trust in the living God, who is the savior of all men, especially those who believe" – I Timothy 4:10b.

"And if anyone sins, we have an advocate with the Father, Jesus Christ the righteous. And He Himself is the propitiation for our sins, and not for our sins only but also for the sins of the world." – I John 2:1-2.

"He sifts as a refiner and purifier of silver." - Malachi 3:3

DISCUSSION QUESTIONS

How do you feel about what you've just learned about the doctrine of hell?

What do you think the baptism of fire is?

How would your life change if you no longer feel the threat of hell and discover that God's purpose for you is far better than you ever imagined?

Can you see why Jesus won't return until His gospel of the kingdom is taught in every nation?

CHAPTER THREE

THE AWESOME AMAZING MYSTERIES OF HIS INCREDIBLE KINGDOM

"Do not be afraid, little flock, for your Father has been pleased to give you the kingdom" (Luke 12:32).

"Again, the kingdom of heaven is like a merchant looking for fine pearls" (Matthew 13:45).

WHAT IF YOUR DAD WAS THE KING of a vast kingdom and he loved you more than anything? What if everything you desired in life, not just material things but also deeper heartfelt experiences like love, peace, joy, wholeness, purpose and fulfillment were within your grasp right now? Let's go even further:

What if you were part owner of such a marvelous miraculous Kingdom?

What if Jesus meant it when He said the poor in spirit are blessed because God's Kingdom is theirs (Matthew 5:3, NAS)? What if you could dramatically improve the lives of countless other people including your loved ones in a way that is uniquely suited to you and them: a way that would fulfill you and them like nothing else can? And what if you could use your spiritual gifts and talents to make the world a better place? These are just some of the awesome biblical benefits of living like a precious child of the King of kings. As a teenager, I read a story about a man who had a special gift. He had a unique uncanny ability to help all who came to him discover what they were created to be and do; to determine the vocation that would most fulfill them. In the story, if a man was working as a mechanic but he was better suited to being a dentist, the man with the special gift could tell him this. That man's whole life would be transformed by that precise bit of knowledge. ***That's exactly what God has promised to you and me.*** As we follow His Spirit, He leads us to discover a perfect fit for our life so that our hopes and dreams work in complete cooperation with God's ways to make the world a better place (See Jeremiah 29:11-14).

Frederick Buechner said it best when he quoted John Eldredge from his book *Wild at Heart*: "We find our vocation (true purpose) where our deep joy and the world's deep needs come together."

Jesus captured our quest for abundance, fulfillment and meaning in his own personal mission statement. He didn't say He came to make us religious nuts. He also didn't say he came to take us to heaven before things on earth get tough. Forgive me for repeating this often but it's some of the best news I've ever heard. I can't get too much of it, and neither can you. Jesus said he came to earth to give us "life, life more abundantly" (John 10:10).

In today's religious climate we can easily misconstrue this. Think with me again about the verse in the Bible we see on signs held aloft at sports games -- the omnipresent John 3:16: "For God so loved the world that He gave His only begotten Son, that whoever believed in him would not perish." (It conspicuously does not say, 'would not go to hell.) It then says, "... but would have eternal life." It conspicuously does not say 'would go to heaven.'

So what exactly is this abundant eternal life Jesus talked about; this unique quality of life so spectacular that God would send His Only Son to earth to die so we could receive it? In one of His greatest promises to us, God said "If He didn't withhold even His own precious Son from us, won't He freely give us all good things to *enjoy*?" (Romans 8:32).

To better understand this abundant life – this eternal life He offers us, let me ask you a question. Would you agree that there are people who are alive but not really living? Listen to Wallace Wattle's poignant description of the people I call the living dead. "Why do you think it is that so many people live mediocre lives, without ever achieving anything of much benefit to the world as a whole? The reason is simply this.....People conform, and the group that most people conform to are the ones that never achieve much in their lives!" So sad but true. He continues: "There are two kinds of people in the world, those who count and those who do not. The vast majority are of those who do not count. They are born; they grow to maturity; they eat, drink, sleep and work; they marry and are given in marriage; they laugh and are happy, and they are sick and miserable in turn; they die, and except as they leave behind them children to do as they have done it is as if they had never lived at all. They are the children of circumstance, the creatures of environment. Their lives are ordered for them by custom and habit; they think the same thoughts and mimic the exact actions of those with whom they chance to be associated. They exercise no power beyond that which is common to their fellows; they leave no footprints on the sands of time. When the census is taken they are counted; but in so far as a really distinct individuality is concerned they do not count. It would answer as well to take their census in blocks of ten as one by one; or to reckon them by the hundred like sheep, for sheep have almost as much individuality as they do. They may be more or less happy, more or less useful, more or less successful; but even if they gain wealth they do not count, for their riches do not give them a distinct personality."

Many of these people even go to church each week, but just as going to a garage doesn't make you a car, going to church doesn't make you a Christian. Most churches merely offer people huge piles of words each week – words based on their particular understanding of right doctrine. And make no mistake, truth is important. Without it we can be led far astray from God's purpose and wonderful plan for our lives. But as John Eldredge says, our eternal judgment isn't based on some celestial SAT Test. Believing the right things about God won't get you into heaven and it certainly won't give you eternal abundant Life. After all, Satan believes true things about God but at least he's smart enough to tremble at the thought.

When Jesus said it's our heavenly Father's good pleasure to give you His kingdom (Luke 12:32), He was talking about making you a joint heir to His Father's Kingdom (James 2:5). Isn't that an astonishing thing to wrap your mind around? The King of kings wants to share His kingdom with us. Now that's really good news! You can be a prince or princess in the supreme Kingdom of the King of kings. And when you finally link up with your eternal destiny, it does more for you and others than anything any amount money can buy.

When I was a young boy, one of the most popular TV shows was *THE MILLIONAIRE*. A multimillionaire named John Baresford Tipton sent a servant out each week to find a deserving person and give him or her a million dollars. More often than not, the money actually harmed the person. However, our heavenly Father's bequest – your incredible inheritance from Him – will not harm you. He promises it will make you immeasurably better.

Where it All Starts

This journey into our highest calling begins with discipleship. As a new Christian I was fortunate enough to be discipled by a wonderful pastor named Warren Campbell. I often refer to him as Santa Claus without a beard. Everywhere he went he radiated love and good cheer, spreading kindness, joy and happiness to every person he encountered; even the clerk who sold him a pack of gum. I worked side by side with him often for 18 hours a day for almost two years, running an inner city youth outreach in Cleveland called Campus Challenge. I knew him as a close friend and spiritual father for many years until his death. I can never recall hearing one unkind or even impatient word cross his lips.

When Warren died, his casket was placed in a church that they kept open around the clock. For days and nights people came from all over the US to pay their respects and testify to what God had done in their life because of him. One of his long time friends said at his funeral, "It was said of Will Rogers that he never met a man he didn't like, but I say to you, Warren Campbell never met a man who didn't like him!"

Warren used to quote a beautiful proverb to me -- one now indelibly imprinted in my mind: ***"The blessing of the Lord maketh rich, and He adds no sorrow to it"*** (Proverbs 10:22). That's how God is when He blesses us. When we receive the extraordinary wealth of His Kingdom gospel, it comes without the sorrow that often accompanies those who become rich in this world's wealth, but lack a rock solid spiritual foundation for their lives (Luke 12:19-20).

Jesus promised His disciples that He would reveal to them the mysteries of His kingdom (Luke 8:10). He said the real reason He spoke in parables was not to make things easier to understand, as is commonly believed, but rather to hide deep spiritual truth from those who had no intention of obeying. He only revealed the mysterious meaning to those who sought after Him for understanding and were willing to obey.

We may wonder why He hid it like that. The Old Testament is full of stories of the sons of kings who inherited their earthly father's kingdom. If his dad followed God closely, obeying God's laws and teaching the people to do the same, the kingdom prospered. But if he died and his son didn't follow his father's example, the whole kingdom suffered greatly, usually by being conquered and enslaved to other nations. Training the king's kids was an extremely important duty. It's equally essential today for the King of kings kids.(I wrote the book *Precious Pearls* to help you do exactly that.)

My first real understanding of the Bible started in a similar way. As a teenager, I attended a church whose pastor didn't believe the Bible literally or disciple anyone. His only 'gospel' was liberal social justice nonsense. But they had a great youth group. (After I became a Christian, I was told by an elder there that the Senior Pastor seduced many of the wives of the elders!)

Prior to surrendering my life to Jesus, I tried to read the King James Bible for many years. With no one to help me understand it, I found it to be a dull, incomprehensible tome. The pseudo-science they teach in public schools made far more sense.

In college, my life got even more messed up. Before I turned 23, I had tried everything I could think of to find happiness. All the world's allures, from drugs, money, a beautiful girlfriend to lots of women and high dollar expense accounts. All that left me a broken, devastated, sad sorry atheist standing on the precipice of suicide. Finally I realized I had never tried God on His terms. I didn't even know what they were. I cracked open the old King James Bible my grandmother had given me years earlier and dared to defy God "If You're there, speak to me. If it makes sense, whatever this book says I will do."

I began reading the red letters (the words of Jesus) in the gospel of Matthew. By the time I got half way through the Sermon on the Mount it all made sense. That night, I gave Him my grimy, self- destructive life, and He began that deep powerful inner revolution that changes everything about us. Had I not done that, had He not shown me the great good news of His Kingdom that night, I doubt I would have lived another 24 hours. I had already decided where to buy the gun I would use to shoot myself in the head.

Jesus Made Many Awesome Promises to Us Concerning God's Kingdom

With His help we can both see it and enter His Kingdom (John 3:3-5). It is within and among us (Luke 17:21). If you seek His Kingdom and righteousness first, you shall have everything else you ever need (Matthew 6:33-4). The quest for His Kingdom will lead you into a dynamic exhilarating experience of righteousness (Romans 14:17) which alone can fulfill us (Matthew 5:6). With all of that, we will also receive lasting love, effervescent joy (John 15) and a personal peace so profound that it surpasses our ability to even comprehend it (Philippians 4).

So how do we get this eternal life that abounds with such amazing benefits? How do we know we are heirs of His Kingdom? In his first epistle, the apostle John tells us: if we abide in Jesus and our Father in heaven, we ***have*** eternal life (I John 2:24-27). We can do this just by doing His will instead of our own (verse 17). And His will is summed up in the commandments to love, for he or she who loves "is born of God" (I John 4:7). It actually makes sense: when we love, we live with an abiding intimate sense of the Presence of the God who IS Love.

Finally, Jesus said that He will only return to earth after this great good news of God's Kingdom has been proclaimed to all the world (Matthew 24:14). Sadly, this gospel of God's Kingdom is hardly being proclaimed even in America yet. But thankfully, he's offered us every key we need to open the doors of our heart and mind to God's incredible Kingdom.

Join me as we examine those keys of the Kingdom together and learn how to use them. We'll explore all of the most important kingdom passages in the Bible and examine what they mean for us. We'll also seek to understand how we can receive all these blessings that will so enrich and transform our life. Then we'll probe all the various parables Jesus taught to expose and examine the amazing Kingdom mysteries.

I'm persuaded that no other study will do more to enhance and deepen our knowledge of God and transform our very lives. He promises us nothing less than to bring heaven to earth (Matthew 6:10) -- to make the very quality of life that people enjoy in heaven a key part of our temporal reality in this life. This is what a friend of mine calls a ***NOW* Heaven**. Want some?

> *"The kingdom of heaven is like treasure hidden in a field. When a man found it, he hid it again, and then in his joy went and sold all he had and bought that field." - Matthew 13:44*

> *"But seek first the kingdom of God and His righteousness and all these things shall be added unto you." – Matthew 6:33*

DISCUSSION QUESTIONS:

Is this kingdom inheritance worth everything you have?

____

____

____

____

____

____

____

____

____

What specific blessings draw you to it?

____

____

____

____

____

____

What do you currently seek first, above and beyond His Kingdom?

____

____

____

____

____

____

How's that working for you?

____

____

____

____

____

____

CHAPTER FOUR

JESUS' DIVINE OBSESSION? HIS POTENT BLOODLINE

"And you shall call His name Jesus, for He will save His people from their sins." – Matthew 1:21b

"And Simon Peter answered Him and said, 'You are the Christ, the Son of the Living God.'" – Matthew 16:16

BIBLICAL NAMES ARE EXTREMELY IMPORTANT. They signify the meaning of a person's life and define his purpose and destiny. Abram's name was changed to Abraham because, as the father of faith, he also became the father of many nations (Genesis 17:5). After he acknowledged who Jesus is, Simon became Peter (Mark 3:16). He was no longer a little stone but the solid rock upon which Jesus built His church. Saul, the persecutor of the early church became the beloved and brilliant Apostle Paul, who authored 13 of the 22 books in the New Testament. The

Old Testament prophets had names that related to their destiny and calling. And every reborn Christian is given a new name (Revelations 2:17). They have a new purpose and value because of their eternal identity and lineage.

Jesus didn't need a new name. His came packed with purpose and significance that's uniquely related to God's Kingdom. However, though we sing about His blessed and holy name and designate denominations, churches, and ministries after it, few of us know what the "name above all names" actually means. And most have never even considered the profound implications His name holds for each of us.

Jesus - Yeshua in Hebrew - is Joshua in the Old Testament, the guy who conquered the giants to give God's people the Promised Land. One reason our Lord was named Jesus is because He would save us from the inner giants of our sins (Matthew 1:28). Notice it doesn't say He would be named Jesus because He would save us from hell or take us to heaven. It also doesn't say He would save us from ***sin***. It says He will save us from sins – plural. He saves us from our specific self-destructive sins. He doesn't just save us from the principle of sin he rescues us from sin's power to harm and destroy our health, well being and even our very life.

Why do we need to be saved from our sins? How can our sins hurt us so much that God Himself would pay such a high price to save us from them? We find some clues to understanding this when we dig deeper into Jesus' name sake Joshua. He led God's people out of the scary, barren, howling wilderness and into the land of abundance God promised them. The Jews went from being slaves in a sparse arid desert to being free people with their own inheritance – a lush fertile land bursting with everything they could possibly want. This land of milk and honey was so rich that the cows dripped milk and the bees oozed honey. This new land didn't just provide for their basic needs it had all that was essential to finally satisfy their deepest heart's desires (Cf.Psalm 37).

There was only one problem with this beautiful fruitful land. It was inhabited by ferocious giants and other powerful godless tyrants who all loved that land and refused to give it to the Jews just because they were God's chosen people. In order for the Jews to receive their inheritance, Joshua had to help them conquer their new enemies. Against overwhelming odds, and with God's omnipotent help and omniscient guidance, he subjugated all their enemies so that His people could totally possess it. Every family then got their own piece of this Promised Land, a personal *inheritance* that they could call their home.

The life of the Jews in the Old Testament is a prescient harbinger that foreshadowed the Christians' Promised Land. As the Jews were enslaved in the literal land named Sin, we are likewise in bondage before we each give our life to Christ. Just as the Hebrews had to traverse a hazardous wilderness to get to their ultimate destination, so also must we embark on a journey that purges us from the things that keep us from receiving the abundant new life He has for us. Deuteronomy 8 explains the divine design for the Jews and us and the purpose of the wilderness in their lives and ours. Why did it take 40 years to travel what should have taken only 18 months? A whole generation that yearned for their past slavery had to die out before a new generation could fight to win the best God had for them.

We have a land of promise also. The Promised Land of the Jews was a precursor to our inheritance of God's Kingdom. Like the Jews, we also have many giants to kill in order to enter and possess God's Kingdom and receive our true inheritance as His beloved children. If the secret sins of alcohol abuse, drug abuse (prescription and illicit), and sex, or work addiction don't get you, the abuse of food most likely will. Most of America is now dangerously overweight. It is great news that through His indwelling Spirit, Jesus conquers the giant self-destructive sins and compulsions that would otherwise rob us of a long abundant life. Jesus became our Joshua to help us do exactly that.

Not all our sins involve chemicals or substances or even immoral activities. After leading spiritual growth and healing retreats since 1980 I totally agree with the Bible that the most destructive organ of the body is the tongue (James 3:5-8). Words can kill or bring life, and they can cause more harm to the soul than anything else the devil can tempt us with. Sins of the flesh harm our bodies but sins of the spirit - rage, bitterness, condemnation and emotional torture and abuse - pollute our very souls and can immeasurably harm those we love the most. You'll read more about this in the chapter on the 43 deadly sins that can steal our Kingdom inheritance. That's why sins like gossip are as bad in God's sight as murder and adultery (Romans 1:29-30). This explains why the Bible's great catalogue of destructive "works of the flesh" includes items like hatred, jealousy, outbursts of wrath, contentions, dissensions, and envy (Galatians 5:19-20).

All sins whether rooted in selfish carnal gratification or inner turmoil and relational antagonism will erode our well-being and damage our very heart and soul. It's wonderful news that Jesus can save us from the inner giants that would steal and plunder our inheritance in God's Kingdom. No wonder Jesus was named as our savior from sins, our Yeshua to lead us to our inheritance of His Kingdom. His very name contains more wonderful divine benefits for this life as well as the next.

The designation of our Lord as the Christ is just as significant as the name Jesus. It literally means Messiah, the Anointed One. King's, prophets and priests were all anointed. This anointing entailed the use of warm oil poured on their head to symbolize the fact that the one being anointed needed the warm power from above - the anointment of God's Spirit - to accomplish his task. Without God's help, each of these three difficult jobs were humanly impossible.

As the King of kings, the ultimate prophet of God and our eternal High Priest, Jesus was all three: the greatest prophet who ever lived, the King of all the kings on the entire earth, and our eternal high priest. However, in a passage I call His inaugural address Jesus gave a talk that almost got Him killed. It also launched his enormous public ministry. Jesus didn't stress the above three functions as the reason for His anointing. Instead, quoting Isaiah 61, he said the reason for His anointing was to ***empower Him to help us with six specific things that all have to do with this life.*** He said He came to heal our brokenness (so we have the necessary strength to become whole and overcome our own inner giants); to free us from our bondage (to sin), liberate us from the power of our wounds (that addict us), heal our inner blindness (so we can see His Kingdom)and receive great news that impacts our deepest poverty. Finally He proclaimed our own personal year of Jubilee (See Luke 4:16-18). This Jubilee was a year long celebration that came every 49 years (Cf. Leviticus 25). Once in every person's lifetime, during this 'acceptable year of the Lord,' all personal debts and obligations were forgiven. If a family had to sell off their piece of the Promised Land to pay their debts, it reverted back to them in the Jubilee year. That way, every Jewish family retained their inheritance in the Promised Land.

What does this mean for us? As I said, the only gospel Jesus proclaimed was the great good news of God's Kingdom (Luke 4:43 and 29 other passages). He also said that His Kingdom is ***within and among*** us (Luke 17:21). He said it wasn't just a matter of keeping certain legalistic club house rules dealing with external matters like food and drink (Romans 14:17), but rather it granted us righteousness, peace and joy in the Holy Spirit (IBID.).

The biblical word for peace is shalom, a glorious word pregnant with promises of favor, blessing, wholeness, well-being, prosperity, tranquility and health. We don't need to wait until we die to taste God's Kingdom and all its inherent blessings. Eternal life begins here and now (John 17:3).

Years ago, at a concert, I was asked to introduce a classic rock music giant in Cleveland. Many won't remember him. His name? Barry McGuire. He sang in a few big bands back in the 60's, but his solo hit **EVE OF DESTRUCTION** became the ultimate rock anthem for 'boomers'. That night, he had recently become a Christian and the eager auditorium was packed with 'Jesus freaks' and other enthusiastic Christians. After I introduced him, I'll never forget his opening words. In his gravelly raspy voice he asked, "How many of you are believers?" The adoring crowd leapt to their feet screaming, whistling and shouting praises. When they quieted down so he could start the music he leaned into the mic and said, "I don't care if you're believers, I wanna be with ***knowers***!" The stunned crowd stared in pregnant silence and the music started for a rapt and eminently attentive audience. Everyone was all ears after that.

As we get to know the Lord intimately, we realize that when we join God's family, God becomes our benevolent heavenly Father and Jesus our beloved big Brother. Both can also become our marvelous eternal Friends. It's only because of what Jesus has done that we can be reborn into God's family (Galatians 4:1-7), and that's the only way to secure our both eternal and temporal inheritances. We must be reborn to become God's cherished children and joint *heirs* with Christ (Romans 8:17). Only then can all that is His becomes ours. Our Promised Land is His Kingdom and in this life we begin to receive all the blessings it bestows on us as heirs of the King of all kings (Galatians 4:30). This is exactly how God's Kingdom truly brings heaven to earth (Matthew 6:10). FYI, if you don't know if you're born again you aren't. The difference in your life is literally night and day, the same as it is when a newborn infant exits the blinding darkness of the womb to enter the brilliant light of a whole new life. Jesus opens our blind eyes and we can truly see everything as it really is.

Here's another way the family metaphor works: when a woman marries she takes a new name. She also receives a portion of whatever her husband has. We do that as Christ's betrothed bride, which is the dominant image used to describe our relationship to Him. *Lord isn't just a synonym for God, it also means husband.*

Adoption is yet another powerful reality that defines our new relationship with God. When a family adopts a child, the child gets a new name - his parent's - and he can enjoy all that his new parents have. As God's adopted children, we too receive our portion from our Father in heaven (Galatians 4:7,30).

This explains why the Christian portion of the Bible is called the New Testament. ***It's a covenant that describes our will and testament. God disclose the promises of our inheritance as joint heirs with Christ and explains the conditions we must fulfill to obtain those promised blessings.*** Who's reborn? Those who follow God's Spirit (Romans 8:14-17). When we die to self and take up our cross daily to follow Him it's because we now know Him personally and His wonderful intentions for us. We fully trust Him and as His disciplined disciples we inherit far more than the Hebrews did when they just received physical property.

To go even deeper, let's examine the richest significance of the blood of Christ. Many people talk about the blood of Christ but very few understand or receive its greatest blessings. In a very real sense, when we submit to His Lordship, His Spirit animates our dead lifeless spirit. Once we welcome Jesus into our heart He becomes one with us. We literally receive the same divine Holy Spirit of God that impregnated His human mother Mary. The selfsame Spirit that birthed Jesus abides in our innermost being when we yield to Him control over our life (John 1:12). ***Once we become His, we become a part of His divine bloodline.*** That's why all that He has is now ours.

Satan worshipers through their secret societies also understand the essential nature of people's bloodlines. Fritz Springmeier explained this brilliantly in his book *The Illuminati Bloodline, The 13 Families that Rule the World*. The 'elite' would have sex with cousins to produce children within their bloodline!

But God has a far more potent bloodline, one that is empowered to truly reign in life and rule the world (Cf. Genesis 5 and Romans 5). This is why our Father's good pleasure is to give us His Kingdom (Luke 12:32). Once we have God's Kingdom, what more can we possibly want?

Years ago, Ron Wyatt, a famous Christian archeologist made an awesome discovery concerning God's Kingdom bloodline. It exposed the scientifically verifiable reality of God's bloodline that is passed down to us through Jesus.

When Wyatt was allowed to explore the rocks beneath Golgotha, the very spot where Jesus was crucified, he discovered a hidden cave. Incredibly, it sheltered the missing Ark of the Covenant. Even more stunning: there was blood on the mercy seat of the Ark!

Wyatt was granted permission to test the blood in a prestigious science lab in Israel. They discovered something more shocking even than the missing Ark. Normal human DNA includes 23 chromosomes from the mother and 23 from the father. The DNA he found on the Mercy Seat far transcended mere humanity. ***The Father's DNA only had one chromosome!*** Even many Jewish rabbis in Israel now believe that this was the actual blood of Jesus Christ. This scientifically proved that God through the Holy Spirit was His Father! There are people who deny this happened but his wife retained the convincing evidence after Ron died.

The implications for us are massive. As a person yields control of his life to the Lordship of Christ (John 1:12) and agrees to follow His Spirit (Romans 8:14), he is born of God. ***This is what I call Followship, and it's essential if we want to fully receive our divine inheritance.*** When you are determined to be Spirit led as Jesus was, God literally becomes your heavenly Father. That's the proof that you have been reborn; that what makes you a true heir to the Kingdom of God. It also makes you teachable so you can handle the responsibilities that come with such a calling. Don't get me wrong. I'm not saying we are not saved by grace, but we are saved for a reason: to do the unique good works which God ordained for each of us (Ephesians 2:8-

10).

What are the Implications? No matter how hellish your earthly father may have been, you now have a Heavenly Father you can trust as Abba, daddy. Your close relationship with Him can undo the works of the devil to harm your childhood and heal all the damage that was done (Read Jeremiah 30). This is an important way that Jesus heals your broken heart and frees you from bondage.

The children of Royals are expected to behave differently from regular citizens, but that's only part of the story. Because the Bible is true Truth, it's only through obedience that you are enabled and empowered to fully partake in the blessings of King's children. When you live to please your Heavenly Father, He bestows His favor upon you. It's impossible for your not to have a blissful and abundant life. As certainly as curses are an inevitable consequence of iniquity, biblical obedience magnetizes God's blessings and they are drawn to you.

This was illustrated for me beautifully by a dear friend who had two NDE's (Near Death Experiences) where she actually visited Heaven. The Lord allowed her to ask any question she wanted. She asked Him to explain sin to her. ***He said "Sin is not fulfilling the purpose I intended for you." Consequently, you fall short of living gloriously!***

The passage I mentioned in Ephesians 2 says we are God's workmanship, but that translation doesn't do it justice. Much of the Bible is written in poetic form but it's hard to grasp in the English Bible. In the original language, 'workmanship' means we are each literally his *Poiema*: his beautiful living poems. Here's where I'm going with this:

Jesus was the Word made flesh. Someone said His Church is the epitome of His creative expression: more glorious even than the Grand Canyon.

There is only one reincarnation taught in the Bible. As certainly as Jesus was the Incarnation of God the Father and His perfect love, we reincarnate Jesus by obeying His commandments which are summed up in the word love.

Now let's go back to consider scriptural legalese. The New Testament is an eternally binding legal document. Again, consider what a last will and Testament represents. It determines the inheritance that heirs receive after the person dies who signed that agreement. When you allow Jesus to be Your Lord, He becomes your big Brother and God becomes your heavenly Father. We can even make a case that the Holy Spirit, which is in the feminine gender in Hebrew and personified so in Proverbs, in essence becomes your heavenly Mother, your comforter; the *Paraclete*: the helpmate who draws parallel alongside of you to teach you all you need to know and to strengthen and help guide you with everything. You have literally been reborn into a whole new family. You've been adopted into the family of the King of kings: a real offspring of His royal bloodline. And since life is in the blood, His royal spiritual blood has now given birth to you spiritually.

The implications are again mind blowing. Few comprehend why Jesus is the second Adam. Through Him, Adam's curse is reversed. Had He sinned just once, He would have failed in His mission, but though Satan tempted Him like no man had ever been tested, He didn't fail! His sinless life thus opened the door to the eternal tree of life for us. You will never die. The same Spirit that raised Jesus from the dead dwells in you. Everything Jesus had now becomes yours. You received it when He died and rose again to help you enjoy investing and spending your new life.

Once we are en-grafted in to Gods family, we receive massive benefits. He who freely gave us His only begotten Son *will not withhold any good thing from us* (Romans 8:32). Through taking on the name of God, what's His becomes ours. Every need, body soul and spirit, is fulfilled (Philippians 4:19). Even our heart's desire becomes attainable (Psalm 37:4-5). And once we have Him living inside of us, He also grants us the power to heal every disease, overcome every demon, and drive out every inner enemy that would seek to steal our rightful inheritance (I Thessalonians 5:23).

So why don't more people experience this incredible life that God promised us? A big part of the reason for this is the way people are 'evangelized.' Most are only taught a severely limited portion of God's good news so when they are introduced to Jesus, ***they received a partial gospel***.

This is why I labored in the first chapter to explain the misunderstandings that most of us have about eternal life. In today's world, most evangelism centers on what I call cheap fire insurance. Contrast this with what Dietrich Bonhoeffer called costly grace. Those who are evangelized are usually told that if they just believe Jesus is God's Son and accept Him as their Savior they will go to heaven and escape hell. U.S. Christians are often taught that when the Great Tribulation comes upon the earth, Jesus will air lift them out. Many are also taught that feelings and spiritual rebirth don't matter; all that matters is intellectually accepting Jesus as their savior. It's almost as if He's standing hat in hand begging us to let Him in.

The main problem with this unbiblical form of evangelism is that it's not what Jesus offered people. Remember, the only good news He proclaimed and sent His disciples to preach was the great news of God's Kingdom (Luke 9:2, etc.). That's why He never clubbed 'sinners' with the hell hammer or baited them with far off Heavenly rewards. He actually only warned religious hypocrites about hell. And He encouraged sinners to repent of their sins so that worse things wouldn't happen to them.

So why shouldn't we mention hell to 'sinners'? We might well ask why Jesus didn't. First of all, most people don't believe they have done anything worthy of hell. John Dillinger, one of the most notorious gangsters in our nation's history, thought he was a good guy. Adolf Hitler considered himself to be the father and savior of the German people.

When we tell people they will go to hell without Christ they develop serious questions about God's justice. Most consider themselves to be good people. How could a just God send them to hell let alone their loved ones who have died without knowing Christ? The 'turn or burn' approach to sharing the gospel has done far more to alienate people than to turn them on to the risen Christ. When evangelism is done this way, very few people make life-changing commitments to Christ.

If the only gospel Jesus shared was the good news of God's Kingdom, we'd best do the same. In fact, ***it's the only way His Kingdom can ever be brought to earth.***

Another major problem with provocative fear based evangelism is that it seldom leads to a new birth experience. In his awesome book *The Greatest Thing in the World*, Henry Drummond, a scientist friend and colleague of the famous evangelist Dwight Moody, criticized what he called offering people 'justification without regeneration'. Most evangelism pushes people into a brief sinner's prayer and then uses one Bible verse ripped out of context to convince them they are saved and heaven bound. This is what I was taught to tell new 'converts' at Billy Graham crusades. What we should be doing instead is help them become truly born again. Only then can they ***see*** the Kingdom, only then can they enter and receive it (John 3:3-5).

Years ago, I was asked to consult with an evangelical mega church. Though they boasted over 10,000 people at their meetings each week, it was obvious to one of the pastors that their men's group was dull and spiritually dead. I asked one of the elders what percent of their people were truly born again. He hadn't a clue. I asked what percent of their elders had ever discipled anyone. Again he had no idea, but he guessed very few. Probably most pastors and elders, even in seemingly thriving congregations, would respond the same.

Rebirth causes radical change. It means that a sweeping, powerful spiritual transformation has taken place. The difference between a fetus in the womb and a newborn child is huge. It's the vast difference between perpetual dependency and becoming a viable human being; between having the capacity to grow to full stature and being forever left in the dark, stunted and inhibited.

Sadly, I fear that few have been presented with the full facts of God's glorious Kingdom. Fewer still have been properly discipled to the point of a genuine rebirth. Consequently, most who consider themselves Christians may be either spiritually still born or severely premature infants who soon die off spiritually. Some are unwittingly aborted or forever spiritually retarded. At best their growth and fruitfulness are hindered. Without the Holy Spirit they can neither recreate the fruits of the Spirit of lead others to be reborn too. I'd be afraid to ask how many Christians in America have ever become spiritually fruitful by discipling anyone.

I stress these points because I'm convinced that we talk much too glibly about heaven and hell. That's precisely why most Christians are uncomfortable evangelizing. They also have a hard time believing the fundamentalist's pitch let alone selling it to friends, relatives and neighbors. And well they should: ***it isn't the awesome comprehensive gospel Jesus proclaimed.***

So what is the essence of eternal life? It's far more than just living forever. Eternal life begins long before we reach heaven or hell. It is a quality of life that surpasses any other way to live on earth. William Barclay, the popular Bible commentator, says ***'Eternal life is living the life God lives.'***

God's GRACE is so much greater than we think.

A simple web search on the original meaning of grace in the Bible yields priceless dividends. In the Old Testament, the Hebrew the word for grace is *HEN* or *HENNON*. It's first mentioned in Genesis 6:8 concerning Noah, ***who's efforts not only saved his whole family but also the entire human race and all animal life on earth!*** Psalm 6:2 describes grace as mercy and illustrates this through Hannah (11th century BC) who's name is derived from *hennon* means ***favor and grace***. Here we see grace as much more than pardon and mercy means more than forgiveness. Together the two words mean ***lovingkindness, favor and relief from stress***.

Hannah's husband had two wives and favored her, but she was still deeply depressed. She was childless, which was a great burden for a wife then. Finally, she promised that if God gave her a son she would devote him to the God as a disciplined Nazarite, where Jesus was later raised. Besides the blessings of mercy favor, lovingkindness and purpose she received all of these blessings as well as her son Samuel, the prophet for whom two Bible books are named. These were all free gifts from almighty God (Exodus 34:6-7). Psalm 145:8-9 further also describes grace as compassion.

In New Testament Greek we see grace (*Charis* or *Charisma*) as even more amazing. It's depth is awe inspiring. Yes, God's righteous law came from Moses and His grace through Jesus (John 1:16-17), but not to disparage the law. ***Rather it empowers us to obey the law***

(See Romans 6-8). Commentator Matthew Henry calls grace "the fullness of Christ in us" that renders us "strong, holy, useful and happy!" It reflects God's good will toward us and in us, including and exuding His divine favor. The Greek Lexicon further defines grace as ***"merciful kindness that turns us to Christ, keeps us in Him and strengthens and increases our faith, knowledge, affection and Christian virtues. Now THAT'S some Amazing Grace!***

How do we do find it? How do we know God and Jesus that intimately? The Apostle John said "As many as received Him (Christ), to them He gave the right and power to become children of God. To those who believed in His name: who were born, not of blood, nor of the flesh, nor of the will of man, but of God" (John 1:12-13). This is what the New Testament covenant is all about. As Jesus' last will and testament, it explains the *inheritance* that becomes ours at His death.

It then shows us how best to spend our inheritance. Jesus rose from the dead to enjoy it with us. When you understand that, Easter becomes your favorite holiday, for it celebrates everything His death gives us. As a fabulous bonus, it reminds us of our eternal retirement benefits. And in this life, living giving as Jesus did can make every day Christmas.

That's why I call GRACE
God's Riches At Christ's Expense.

God only promised we would find Him if we seek Him with our whole heart! But when we do that, we find the greatest endowment God can personally bequest to us: God's favor! It begins in this life by transforming us and renewing our entire mind so we can see, think and do as Jesus did!

DISCUSSION QUESTIONS:

What do you think of Jesus' name now?

____

____

____

____

____

____

How do you feel about this Kingdom gospel He proclaimed?

____

____

____

____

____

____

What if anything can keep you from receiving your full inheritance?

How will your life change with this comprehensive understanding of grace?

CHAPTER FIVE

KEY ONE: THE SACRED SECRET TO PROSPERITY

“But seek first the kingdom of God and His righteousness, and all these things shall be added to you.” – Matthew 6:33

Then Jesus said to His disciples, "I tell you the truth, it is hard for a rich man to enter the kingdom of heaven.” - Matthew 19:24

“Blessed is a person who finds wisdom, and one who obtains understanding. For her profit is better than the profit of silver, and her produce better than gold. She is more precious than jewels, and nothing you desire compares with her. Long life is in her right hand; in her left hand are riches and honor.” - Proverbs 3:13-16

WHEN I DECIDED TO WRITE THIS BOOK, I was overwhelmed by the magnitude of the task. As I said, over 150 passages in the New Testament and half of

Jesus' parables explore God's heavenly Kingdom. As I analyzed the data, I discovered there were seven major mysteries buried in all that data; seven distinct keys for entering, inheriting and possessing everything that God's Kingdom has for us. Among them is something we all want and need to resolve: the issues related to financial abundance. After all, Jesus spoke more about money than anyone else in the Bible. A proper understanding of His message is essential if we are to appropriate everything God desires for us.

A wise man once said the Kingdom of God is upside down. We certainly see that in the Beatitudes (Matthew 5:1-12) and other intriguing teachings of Jesus. We're to love our enemies and turn the other cheek when someone hits us. The poor are blessed and the meek inherit the earth. Is it possible Jesus knows what He's talking about? Can we really fight relational fire with water? How in the world can the meek inherit the earth? Everyone wants a bigger piece of the economic pie, even those Christians who shun scriptural prosperity. But who would ever guess that the meek can uniquely manifest it? Even in this verse, when properly understood, God's word makes perfect sense. As we shall see again and again, in this world, the devil hides in the details trying to confuse us. God's word is where we find the cognitive angels who clarify everything. God's Kingdom provides all we will ever need if we embrace its simple yet profoundly sensible conditions.

Is there a Poverty Gospel?

The first confusion we must confront concerns the question of poverty or prosperity. If the poor are blessed, should Christians be rich? Should we have plenty or suffer lack? If money is evil, why strive for more of it? What does God truly want for us? Unless we sort this out, we can't live faithfully in financial matters. What's worse, even if the Lord wants us to experience material prosperity as well as spiritual abundance, that can't happen if we don't believe it's God's will. Faith is the currency of God's Kingdom; we are only guaranteed to receive what we honestly believe (Cf. Mark 9 and 11).

Our confusion may relate to Jesus' statement that the Kingdom is like a hidden treasure (Luke 13:44); that it's the pearl of great price (verse 45). It's so precious that once we find it, we would sell all that we have so we can own it.

When Jesus said He was anointed to preach good news to the poor (Luke 4:18), He said a mouthful - one that further compounds our confusion. Most sincere Christians honestly struggle to understand the proper role of money in our lives. Some believe it is evil to be rich, especially if you're serving Him. After all, didn't Jesus say it's almost impossible for a rich man to enter God's Kingdom (Luke 18:24-5)? Didn't He also say the poor are blessed (Matthew 5:3)? Doesn't the Bible teach that money is the root of all kinds of evil and that we shouldn't trust in the uncertainty of wealth (cf. I Timothy 6:9-10)?

A young man got angry with me as I taught a class on the miracle of tithing. He knew many faithful Christians who were poor. So do I. But some may have chosen poverty like

Francis of Assisi did. Others may have failed to honor God with their tithes and offerings (cf. Malachi 3). Still others may be in a temporary time of poverty through no fault of their own. I made stupid mistakes as a day trader during the dot com collapse and lost two thirds of my net worth in six weeks; stupid because I proudly thought I was a financial genius and never asked God when to buy and sell. I also didn't listen to my wife. Financial poverty can bring us to God and eventually enable us to inherit His Kingdom, but nowhere does the Bible teach that it's a blessing to remain poor. ***Jesus was told to preach the Kingdom gospel to the poor so they could prosper!***

Many scriptures teach us the secrets to prosperity. Just read Proverbs 8. A simple web search can bring up 70 or more such passages. Why would God's Word do that if He wanted us to be poor? Many Christians believe that God wants us to be successful and wealthy. After all, John prayed that above all things we would prosper ***and*** be in health as our soul prospers (III John 2). Weren't King David and Solomon and many other biblical rulers fabulously wealthy? Why do so many scriptures explicitly teach us how to prosper and be successful in all we do (Cf. Proverbs 8:17-21, Joshua 1:6-8)? ***No wonder Soren Kierkegaard felt that the Bible could only be properly understood when seen through the lens of paradox!***

So what is the essence of Jesus' good news for the poor? In one way or another, at certain times in our lives, we are all impoverished, spiritually or materially or both. After teaching scriptural finances for years I felt like a total hypocrite when I had to file for bankruptcy. But once we sort out this wealth issue, it can't help but benefit us and our loved ones greatly. We can finally discover the kingdom key to scriptural prosperity and have more money to spread the Kingdom gospel. Years ago I read that most millionaires file bankruptcy three times before they succeed. That's the only way the year of Jubilee can be implemented in our secular tax system. Oh yeah, Jesus came to preach that Old Testament teaching too.

We've already seen that the only gospel Jesus offers us is the awesome good news of God's Kingdom, so we must first examine what the kingdom passages in the New Testament say about wealth and prosperity.

Poverty or Prosperity: Which is God's Will for You?

First, let's examine what the good news isn't. While Jesus said the poor are blessed, He didn't say "Blessed are the poor for they can receive welfare." Instead, those who are impoverished in spirit and finances are most blessed because the Kingdom can become theirs. But once a poor person opens up to God's Kingdom, once they are born again so they can see and enter it (John 3:3-5), He promises that if they honor the conditions of Kingdom government, He will provide for their every need and desire (Matthew 6:19-34, John15). ***After all, Jesus became poor that we might become rich (II Corinthians 8:9)!*** And He clearly meant rich in all ways, not just rich in spiritual matters. Proverbs is packed with sage advice on how to attain that form of godly wisdom that bestows wealth upon all who understand and honor it. Like any good father, our perfect Heavenly Father delights in our prosperity (Read Psalm 35)!

Above all things, we are to seek first God's kingdom and righteousness (Matthew 6:33). Most 'believers' don't exactly make God's Kingdom their first priority. They usually squeeze God in when they have time. Few people set aside time with Him early in the morning, and every day is poorer because of it (Proverbs 8:17-18). I know this because I've started way too many days on the run, without seeking Him first. And I've poignantly experienced the emptiness and futility of those days. They contrast dramatically with those beautiful days, weeks, months and years when I start each day with meaningful time with Him.

Someone once spoke of the barrenness of a busy life and the busyness of a barren life.

How true. No one can honor God with the first fruits of their labor and become poorer because of it. Tithing - paying ten percent of our income to the Lord's work - is akin to kingdom taxes. This is the bare minimum God expects of His followers (Read Malachi 3:8-12). We don't *give* tithes, we *pay* them because we owe them to God. If we don't pay them *we are robbing Him* (IBID). He doesn't need our money. We are robbing Him of the joy He receives by blessings us!

In addition to our tithes, He also challenges us to give alms to the poor and offerings for special needs and ministries. If we give as God does, ***even other people will give richly to us*** (Luke 6:38). We truly can't out-give God. He expects us to live as if all we own is His (Luke 14:33). Someone once said, "God has a problem, He thinks He's God!"

What would happen if we did this? What if we tell God everything we have is His and mean it? Again, God doesn't need our money. Warren Campbell, my spiritual father, used to say, "God owns the cattle on a thousand hills and the taters in 'em. Whenever I need something He just sells off one of those cows."

A man recently boasted that he had read extra-biblical books that convinced him he didn't have to tithe. He was shocked when I said, "That's right. You don't have to you *GET* too." I looked around the dining room of the home where he rented a bedroom from a lady. He couldn't even afford his own apartment. God commands us to tithe and even do more ***for our own benefit***. Just like the Sabbath, tithing was made for man, not man for tithing. ***In fact, the only place in the Bible where God invites us to test Him is in our finances.*** It's here that He makes His greatest promises concerning wealth. ***He says if we pay our tithes and give our offerings He will open the heavens and pour out such a great blessing that we can't contain it*** (Malachi 3). Yet only three percent of those who claim to be Christian tithe. Only seven percent of those who claim to be Bible believing Christians tithe. Over 50% of pastors don't believe Christians must tithe. No wonder most of us live paycheck to paycheck. It's not God's fault. He's told us how to have more than enough but we won't listen. Friends, God isn't a liar; He always honors His Word, but if we don't do our part He can't do His. God's promises are all conditional. They hinge on our obedient response. And nothing tests your faith or better reveals God's generosity than the mandate to pay our tithes.

But seeking God's Kingdom first means much more than what we do with our money. It means living by the benevolent laws of our King; precepts designed to bless and protect us. And as we've seen, many of these divine directives pertain to money and how we should use it beyond our tithes.

Thankfully, a pastor taught me to tithe when I was a new Christian. As I did that throughout my life, He has consistently multiplied my income and provided resources for me far above the income level I had. My first full time job as a Christian was as editor of an underground Christian newspaper during the days of the Jesus Movement. I lived in a Christian commune in the inner city where we were given the roof over our head, shared communal meals and received car expenses and a salary of $10 a week. My parents thought I was crazy. The first week I lived there, two people offered to take me out to dinner. Both insisted I order lobster! Others donated expensive antiques for my room. I could go on and on about the abundance He provides me as I seek to follow Him and order my finances biblically.

Years later, when I resigned from pastoring a mainline church because the Lord told me to, I thought I'd have to move my family form the parsonage to a house trailer. Instead, I bought my dream house with no money down, no job, no credit and no salary. The day I moved in I got instant equity of $45,000. This was exactly the amount I lost while living in a parsonage for eight years! Time and again I've forsaken all to follow His call. Each time He's generously provided for my every need and even my desires. ***I feel bad for people who have no idea what a great 'advent adventure' it is to live by faith.***

All my life my father justified not tithing because some pastor told him he could tithe with his time. He never gave one tenth of his hours to God and we never got out of poverty, all because he believed he didn't need to honor God with the first fruits of his labors.

Pastors often don't like to talk about money because their people don't like to hear it, but it's a great disservice to their flock. Nothing helps personal and church finances more than tithing and nothing does more to teach us about God's faithfulness. At one point Jesus promises a hundred fold return on our investment in His kingdom (Mark 10:30). No stock broker can guarantee you that. When people tell me they can't afford to tithe, I tell them they can't afford not to.

Once I realized I need to prosper if I am to accomplish all that the Lord intends for my life, I began meditating day and night on my favorite Psalm: ***"Let the Lord be magnified who has pleasure in the prosperity of His servant" (Psalm 35:27, NKJV).*** As I reflected on that passage, I first realized that God doesn't promise to prosper every churchgoer or person who claims to be a Christian. It says He delights in His ***servant's*** prosperity. As I meditated on that verse I soon realized that though I'm not perfect I am certainly His servant. When I die, I want nothing more or less than to hear Him say, "Well done good and faithful servant." Once I acknowledged that, it became easier to believe that He would be happy if I prospered. And doesn't that make sense? I'm blessed when I see my children prosper. How much more is God blessed when we do. Sadly, many think that a pastor is ripping people off if he becomes wealthy even though they help far more people than most secular billionaires.

As I further digested that prosperity passage I saw something else. God's true nature can be ***magnified***. He is not a celestial skinflint. In fact, He is ***magnificently*** generous. And He is seen more easily for how He really is when His servants prosper. As we prosper, people can see that serving the Lord is a blessing that rewards us in this life as well as the next. Nations have proven this throughout history. As countries have lived by biblical values they have prospered. When those values are eclipsed by secular standards, those same civilizations decline. Just look at Europe. Look at the United States today. Whenever a person, church or culture shuns biblical values it doesn't take long for decay (decadence) to set in.

The Bible contains much wisdom about money. Solomon, in all probability the wealthiest man in history, offers us great advice on how to prosper. He said those who seek after wisdom diligently will find it, and will discover that's it's better than anything mere money can buy (Proverbs 8:17). With it come riches, honor and peace. All of wisdom's ways are pleasant and they lead to ***happiness*** (Proverbs 3:13-18). Those who love wisdom are promised rewards that are better than gold and silver, but the rewards also include enduring wealth, righteousness and full treasuries (Vss. 18-21).

Once again, if wealth were evil, why would the Lord show us how to acquire it? ***Money isn't the root of all evil, the love of money is*** (I Timothy 6:10). Money is powerful, but it alone can't exclude the wealthy from God's Kingdom, it must merely be kept in proper perspective. When Jesus said it's easier for a camel to enter the eye of a needle than for the rich to enter His Kingdom He was talking about something every Jew understood. The needle's eye was a small gate into the city that they left open at night for people arriving late. People could enter but attacking armies with all their weaponry could not. The only way a camel could enter this small gate was to unload everything on its back and crawl through on its knees.

Kingdom laws on paying our tithes, giving alms (caring for the poor and needy) and giving additional offerings to ministries as we are led are essential. They help us prosper by making God and people more important than money. Whenever we do that, we receive His supernatural provision. I recently experienced this again. I had forgotten to pay about $70 worth of tithes and my income dried up. Within two days of paying those tithes, over $7,000 dollars was donated 'unexpectedly.' That's a hundred fold increase!

What about clergy? Can they prosper? The Roman Catholic Church requires vows of poverty from its leaders but Jesus didn't. The Apostle Paul says ***God will meet all***

our needs through the abundance of riches we have in Christ Jesus. He also tells us he has personally both been abundantly blessed and suffered extreme financial privation (Philippians 4:12). We may experience both extremes too. I have, but there's no denying that financial provisions and prosperity are a part of God's Kingdom blessings. The Old Testament priests' garbs would cost thousands to duplicate today. Soldiers even bartered over Jesus' robe when He was crucified. My friend who's a bespoke fashion designer said that Jesus' seamless robe would also cost a lot. And by the way, Jesus followers and those who benefited from His ministry supported Him financially (Luke 8:1-3). The Old Testament affirms this. God brought His people into their inheritance in the Promised Land ***to establish His covenant with them (Deuteronomy 8) and to teach them to gain exceptional wealth***, but it came with a steep price, as we'll see later.

God's grace is much bigger than eternal pardon. ***I love this acronym for GRACE: God's Riches At Christ's Expense.*** No passage expresses God's gracious generosity better than this one: ***"For you know the grace of our Lord Jesus Christ, that though He was rich, yet for your sakes He became poor, that you through His poverty might become rich"*** (II Corinthians 2:8). Remember, grace is Charis in Greek. Our word charity comes from it. The charismatic renewal during the Jesus movement used that title. It perfectly describes the selfless love of our living God, who is the embodiment of perfect love. That generous, gracious charitable love was incarnated in His son Jesus the Christ.

There is a false prosperity gospel. It's the so-called law of attraction:; name it and claim it, blab it and grab it. Those who advocate this tell you to plant monetary seeds in their ministry. That's not how Jesus explained it. And sadly, most who use that metaphor, prod people mercilessly to donate to them. Don't fall for it. But don't let that dissuade you from the scriptural prosperity gospel. It always works. Theologians describe scripture as autopistic, which means self- authenticating. It automatically authenticates your faith. God's Word proves it's true once we start obeying it.

"So Jesus answered and said, 'Assuredly, I say to you, there is no one who has left house or brothers or sisters or father or mother or wife or children or lands, for my sake and the gospel's, who shall not receive a hundredfold now in this time – houses and brothers and sisters and mothers and children and lands, with persecutions – and in the age to come, eternal life." – Mark 10:29-31

"And you shall remember the Lord your God, for it is He who gives you power to get wealth that you may establish His covenant which He swore to your fathers, as it is this day" (Deuteronomy 8:18).

"It is the blessing of the Lord that makes rich, and He adds no sorrow to it" (Proverbs 12:22).

DISCUSSION QUESTIONS

Do you want to prosper?

____

____

____

____

____

____

How do you define an abundant life?

____

____

____

____

____

____

____

What must you change to prosper and live life more abundantly?

____

____

____

____

____

____

CHAPTER SIX

KEY TWO: FRUITFULNESS FOR FABULOUS FOLLOWSHIP

"You did not choose me, but I chose you and appointed to that you should go and bear fruit and that your fruit should remain, that whatever you ask the Father in my name He may give you" – John 15:16.

IN THE FIRST PART OF THIS SCRIPTURE, Jesus told us to see yourself as a person who has been chosen. We could even say it defines true Christ followers: we are appointed to be fruitful. This is our raison d'etre; the Christians reason for being. We were chosen to bear lasting fruit. The whole verse doesn't just relate to evangelism but also to every important area of your life. And if you wonder why your prayers are seldom answered with a resounding yes, in the next phrase He gives you the amazing key to answered prayers. All of God's promises, including answered prayer, are conditional: if you do this, He will do that. Astonishingly, Jesus promised that if we abide in Him and become fruitful, ***our heavenly Father will give us whatever we request in His name.***

Our kingdom purpose and fulfillment both come from being who we are, living like ***whose*** we are, and doing what He created us for: we are all created for spiritual reproduction. Instead of ending in the Old Testament, the command to be fruitful and multiply began in a whole new way with Jesus.

A friend once asked me why Jesus cursed the fig tree (see Mark 11). After all, it seemed unjust; figs weren't even in season. I asked her to imagine a farmer with animals, orchards and vineyards. What if his cows didn't give milk, his chickens didn't lay eggs, his sheep didn't grow wool, and his pigs didn't produce baby pigs? What If his apple trees didn't produce apples or all his grapes were sour? He'd be out of business real quick and his investment would be worthless. *When He cursed the fruitless fig tree Jesus gave His disciples an essential visual they would never forget. Jesus had power to even curse a tree.* And He expected all trees His to bear fruit, 'in season and out of season.'

This lesson underscored many things He taught. He said God can do anything, as long as we believe (Mark 11:22-24). He later said we're made new people in Christ so we can spiritually reproduce (John 15:1-8). The vine attached to the branch produces grapes (verse 4). So the earliest biblical command to "Be fruitful and multiply" (Genesis 1:22-28) extends to all Christians once they're reborn. Our very destiny is connected to it, as is much of the good news of His Kingdom. Fruitfulness is a powerful key that unlocks many things for God, His kingdom and for us. First, it enables and empowers the never ending expansion of His Kingdom, just as the Bible predicts (Isaiah 9:7). Next it's the secret to making earth like heaven. For those very reasons it's a major key that unlocks all other benefits of His Kingdom for us through answered prayer. ***That's why this passage contains the sacred secret to getting our Lord to grant our every request!***

And there's another benefit. The thing that attracted Jesus' disciples wasn't escaping eternal damnation. Most Jews didn't believe in that. Remember, in the original language there is virtually no mention of a fiery eternal hell. Instead Jesus also offered them deep meaning and eternal significance; *the possibility of becoming fishers of men* (Matthew 4:19). They could make a real difference in the lives of their loved ones and all people. They could make the whole world a better place. He gave that promise to us as well.

Sadly, most of the Church still hasn't gotten the memo on that wonder filled piece of good news. George Barna did a survey that discovered that in a recent twenty year period the American Church spent 500 billion dollars on itself – that's a half of a trillion dollars – and didn't increase the percent of Americans who are Christians by even one percent. Why? ***I believe that in the partial gospel model that most churches' adopted, pseudo evangelism is the problem not the solution***. The practice of bringing people to church or revival meetings to get saved is unbiblical and ineffective.

As much as I want people to experience a new and wonderful life in Christ, I'm getting to the place where I don't want to see any more alter calls; at least not until we're prepared for them. Lest you tune me out, please allow me to explain. God didn't give pastors or even evangelists to the Church to do all the work for us. ***Shepherds don't reproduce sheep, sheep do.*** We are all called to do the work of an evangelist (II Timothy 4:5). In his book *The Coming Revival*, Bill Bright reported that only two percent of believers in America share their faith in Christ with others. His ministry motto was Come Help Change the World. He wrote a little tract on the four spiritual laws for his converts to use when evangelizing. The problem is that hardly anyone who 'accepted Christ' through that tract stayed Christian or became disciples, but it looked like many thousands were 'converted.'

People must be discipled. The results of not doing this are significant. Approximately 96% of church growth doesn't come from evangelism or discipleship; it comes from nomadic spiritual migration between churches. Some would call that Sheep Stealing. No wonder pastors are reluctant to work with other pastors to advance God's Kingdom!

Let me change gears here and bring in one of the more controversial passages in the Bible. In a seldom quoted verse, we're told that women are saved through childbirth, as long as they persist in faithfulness and purity (I Timothy 2:15). What in the world does this enigmatic verse mean? Certainly it's not saying that single or childless women won't go to heaven. I believe it reveals a far deeper truth. A female friend mentioned to me that at her job, the women who have never married and had children cause real problems. She said they are self-centered, catty, gossipy and mean spirited. They tend to only think of themselves. And I quote her: "Even other women can't get along with them."

This may get to the essence of what that scripture means. When I got married, I wasn't sure I wanted kids. They were messy, expensive, and severely limited our personal freedom. My wife was equally dubious. We weren't going to have any kids for at least five years or until we figured this out. In spite of birth control, the kids started coming. We had four kids in six years! And they were messy, and expensive, and limited our personal freedom! ***But they were also well worth it.*** At least until they turned thirteen. JUST KIDDING! They were all keepers and most days I'd never have traded them in.

Why do I say they were worth it? My answer may surprise you. Children mortify our selfish tendencies; and that's a good thing. Selfishness is counterproductive. It keeps us from understanding the key to true happiness and fulfillment. I thank God for our kids. They did more to teach us to be Christ-like than anything else we could have done. And they brought us far more joy than grief along the way. Nothing causes a woman more pain than giving birth. Nothing destroys a woman's self- centeredness like having children. And the great blessing of birthing and raising children is probably the only thing that could do that. Fortunately, that blessing starts as soon as she holds her child.

And lest you think guys get off easy, let me hasten to say that nothing mortifies a man's self-centeredness like being a biblical husband. I was talking with a Christian woman over brunch one day who told me she was very happy just having a boyfriend; she didn't ever want to get married. I asked why. She said "Cuz I can still do what I want." When I laughed she gave me a dirty look and demanded I explain. After silently praying for some fast wisdom I said "It's true; the Bible teaches women should submit to her husband as to the Lord but men are told to do something far harder." She scrunched up her nose at me. It was too late to turn back now. I pointed to our plates and said, "Consider a bacon and eggs breakfast. The hen makes a donation but the pig makes a sacrifice." She still didn't get it. "The husband is told to love his wife as Christ loved the church. He died for us." She finally got it but she still didn't buy it. Last I knew she's still single and dating the same guy today about fifteen years later.

Why do I have the audacity to open this can of worms? The same principle of dying to self applies to all Christians. Pastors will tell you that most Christians are selfish. They don't usually ask, 'What Would Jesus Do', they ask what will He do for me, endlessly demanding to have their needs met. They whine for better kids programs, or for the church to 'take care of our teens'. They want pastors to entertain them on Sunday with jokes and short sermons. And to make sure the worship is rich and stimulating. When I taught a Bible study in my home people wanted me to talk more and do less discussion.

When I taught at Church they wanted me to talk less and give them freedom to interrupt. "Don't ask us to volunteer," Christians say. Like whiny children, most want their pastors to do more for them, and for Pete's sake, they want us to stop talking about money! That's probably why most pastors today 'don't believe in tithing.' As a young pastor, I asked my church board how may hours they wanted me to spend on sermon prep, Sunday School, hospital visits, youth, Sunday evening prayers service, Wednesday Bible study, leadership training, disciple making, visitor follow up and church administration. It came to 85 hours per week. They finally got it. I could have a real day off, use an answering machine, and get board members and others to help with things.

Self-centeredness quickly changes in Christians who do ministry and have spiritual children. Bearing spiritual children is a lot like having natural ones. And make no mistake here:

When people are born again they must be raised again.

For all Christians, dying to self is not an option it's required. That's the real meaning of baptism. But if we believe the whole Bible, we soon discover that with all kinds of death comes resurrection to a better life. That's the unseen benefit of spiritual childbearing. We know the unique joy of spiritual parenthood *AND* we become more like Jesus. Just like Him, we too endure the cross for the joy of true, deep, intimate fellowship with those whom we raise in the Lord.

As in many enterprises, ten percent of church goers do 90 percent of the work. As a pastor, I preferred working with the ten percent of Christians who were committed. They made it all worth while. Somebody said every church needs a 'back door revival', a different kind of membership drive: one that drives out all the lazy complainers so the church can finally grow.

Many churches grow because they recruit people from other churches. When I pastored a mainline church, a local Pentecostal pastor would take my wealthy members out to lunch so he could tempt them with all that he did right (much of which wasn't scriptural).

As a pastor, I preferred working with people who had no church background rather than those who came from other congregations. ***Spiritual blended families cause even more problems than natural ones.*** I felt like I could raise my own spiritual kids much easier than trying to train those who came from another family. When I didn't have to deal with a blended spiritual family I had far fewer bad habits to undo.

So, what are Pastors for? *Professional clergy exist to equip God's people for building up the Church in love and doing the work of ministry* (Ephesians 4:11-15). Try it. God's ways really work. You might even get hooked. The Apostle Paul said he loved ministry so much he was *addicted* to it (I Corinthians 16:15).

So what's wrong with alter calls? This may shock you, but the church doesn't exist to make converts, it's here to make mature Christians.

God doesn't care about making Decisions for Christ; He wants us making Disciples of Christ

Simply put, if Jesus is not your Lord, He's not your savior. If you don't obey all He commands your aren't a Christ follower. And Jesus wasn't just speaking to Jews. *Paul the apostle to Gentiles said if you don't follow Him you aren't really born again (Read Romans 8:12-14).*

When a friend got back from a mission trip to India she made a fascinating observation. As she listened to an evangelist who offered people salvation, many streamed forward to receive it by saying a simple sinner's prayer. When they he offered people the opportunity to make Jesus Lord, far fewer responded, but during that prayer, demons manifested in almost everyone who made that commitment. They then had to renounce them and cast them out. My friend asked why I thought that happened. My answer shocked her. "Demons don't care if we make converts. Easy- believism just makes people religious, and religion is one of Satan's most effective tools to turn people off to God. But if we make disciples, the demons fight back. It means their reign in a person's life is over and they must leave, for *if Christ possesses a soul, Satan cannot.*" What would happen if we cast all the demons out of people before we baptized them? Better yet, what if we did that before they were allowed to be pastors, elders or board members? I learned that religious spirits are far more evil than any other kind. That's what makes people whiny, judgmental and cantankerous. Who wants to attend a church full of people like that?

I understand why non-Christians believe the lie that religion causes most of the wars and suffering in history. That's only true if we include the religions of atheistic Communism and secular Humanism. *The wars spawned by atheists in the 20th century by people like Stalin, Hitler and Mao killed more people than all the other wars in the entire history of man combined.* But bad religion killed Jesus, and sadly it still seeks to stamp him out today. I'm not just talking about radical Islam my friends, though it has killed many millions of people. While authentic Judaeo-Christian religion won't murder innocents in the name of God, it can inoculate them with just enough phony religion to keep them from getting the real thing. And if you've read the book of Revelations, you know what God does with lukewarm believers (Cf. Rev. 3:14-21). Projectile vomit anyone? And please remember and be very careful when you interpret the end times. We're seriously warned to neither add nor subtract anything said in the book of Revelations (Verses 22:18-19). I sure don't want the curses in Revelations to fall on me.

When Christians judge, condemn and alienate people who don't even know Jesus because they drink or smoke or their sex life doesn't immediately measure up to biblical standards, how do we expect them to respond when the only 'salvation' we offer them is an irrational unbiblical *'turn or burn theology?'* Or when we condemn others because they don't believe exactly the way we do, or when pastors publicly rail against other pastors whose congregations are thriving more than theirs. God isn't impressed. When we strain at spiritual gnats like whether people 'swear or chew or go with girls who do' but swallow the camels of gossip, lovelessness, and holier than thou judgmental-ism, His people are the real problem. Someone once asked a pastor why he didn't teach his members to evangelize. He said he didn't want them to spread their spiritual diseases!

I once saw a pastor who stood up to preach wearing a Tee shirt that said, 'Lord, spare me from Your children'. His jam packed congregation of young Gen Z's (Zoomers not Boomers) roared with laughter.

Most of us are what I call **'burned again' Christians**. Many of us have been more wounded and damaged by the friendly fire of Christian siblings who reject, judge, condemn, betray and backbite than we ever have by worldly people who are often more compassionate. As someone wisely said, any moron can use a wrecking ball, but it takes more time, skill and effort to build something.

Sadly, many people find better 'fellowship', in bars than churches. A new pastor told his elders the address for their first evangelistic training. They all came to it dressed in a coat and tie. When they arrive, they were shocked to see the pastor sitting in in a local bar dressed in jeans and a sport shirt. Looking around at the surprise location and people around them, they pressed the pastor to explain why he chose such a place. His reply: "I wanted you to feel what they would experience if they visit our church."

No Wonder Jesus Befriended Sinners: Look how Religious People Treated Him!

Hypocrisy runs rampant when churches become more like dysfunctional spiritual orphanages than healthy spiritual families. Why? We have focused on conversions instead of transformation, false religion rather than realized righteousness, and superficial club house rules with few if any key Kingdom mandates.

The movement of some pastors to embrace "spiritual formation" intrigued me. It's an attempt to get churches back to helping form Christ's likeness into their members. When I first heard about it, this surprised me because that's what true churches should always do.

If we're to help people become Christ-like, we must return to our true great co-mission with Christ. Everywhere Jesus went He shared the glorious good news of God's Kingdom. That means we must make legitimate disciples instead of just promiscuously propagating more spiritual orphans, especially if we have no intention of raising them to blessed maturity in Christ.

Frankly, our spiritual infant mortality rate is awful. Here are some stunning statistics: according to Charles E. Hackett, National Director of Home Missions for a leading U.S. denomination. He said a soul at the altar doesn't generate much excitement because approximately ninety-five out of every hundred won't become integrated into the church. ***Most will not return for a second visit.***

In 1991, organizers of a Salt Lake City Christian concert encouraged follow-up. They also said less than five percent of those who respond to an altar call during a public crusade are living a Christian life one year later. A mass crusade reported 18,000 decisions for Christ, yet according to Church Growth magazine, ninety-four percent failed to become incorporated into a church. The March/April 1993 issue of American Horizon disclosed the fact that 'In 1991, over 11,500 churches of a major U.S. denomination had obtained 294,784 decisions for Christ. Unfortunately, they could find only 14,337 who continued in fellowship. ***They couldn't account for over 280,000 of those 'decisions!'"***

The determination to follow Christ is the most important decision in anyone's lifetime. It shouldn't be made during an emotional moment over the eminent threat of eternal damnation or the vague promise of heavenly bliss. ***If that were truly God's way to reach people, Jesus would have done so.***

As a young Christian, I learned how fragile simplistic evangelism is and how much harm it can do. I 'evangelized' most of the kids in my junior high youth group only to see almost all of them fall away in a few short months. It's easy to sway young people, but just as easy for someone else to pry them away; and once a person has been inoculated with a little bit of gospel, it's even less likely they will ever catch the real thing. *Many people who want nothing to do with Christ think they already tried that. Most were never truly born again.*

Two years after that youth group experience, I started a Christian coffee house outreach at a vacation resort community. We decided to do things differently. We remained open after the bars closed so we could reach "real sinners" and maybe help some sober up before driving home. I also studied what Jesus said about sharing the good news in a way that produced lasting results. Instead of asking for instant conversions, we just loved people. On each table we had a small card that explained that the coffee, soda and homemade cookies were free because we love Jesus. He also often asked profound questions when He spoke with people, so on the back of the flyer it said, *WHAT IS YOUR RAISON D'ETRE??* We then developed close relationships with sincere seekers, offering to answer any questions they had about God and life, starting with the definition of *RAISON D'ETRE*? (Why are you alive?). When people asked questions we simply showed them scriptures that helped then understand God's reasoning.

Every person's favorite channel is WIFM: What's In it For Me. ***People can only truly obey with their whole heart once they understand why it's in their own best interest (Psalm 119:34).*** With this approach, we had far fewer converts but most became genuine disciples. And over 40 years later, many of those people are still evangelizing and discipling others.

Seed that is rooted in self interest in this life as well as the next bears real fruit. When people see and understand why God's plan for their life makes sense, they will long to become lasting fruit (Cf. Mark 4:1-20, note especially verse 17).

Let's Truly Change the World

Jesus had the most important mission in the universe and only three years in which to accomplish it yet He was never in a hurry. His chief task was to make disciples who would carry on after He was gone. So how did He do that? He carefully chose men to be close to Him every day and showed them Kingdom reality. He let them see how He lived and He answered all their questions. *Sadly, most schools that train pastors teach their students not to let people get close to them so the other parishioner's won't be jealous.*

If every church equipped their people to make disciples, teaching them to obey the simple and profound laws of love that Jesus commanded, the entire country would radically change and America could again help transform the world. But that probably won't happen, so let's be more realistic. *If just ten percent of America's churches trained the committed ten percent of their members to just make one disciple a year and trained that person to do likewise,* ***each church would more than triple in just five years and there would be three times as many committed Christians in America.***

So if we run the numbers, let's say out of three hundred million Americans, half claim to be Christians. (Actually, more like 60 percent do.) Ten percent of that smaller number would be 15 million people. Using this model, in three more years, that would make for over 50 million committed Christians. In two more years that would swell to 150 million. In two more years, almost all of the US would be exposed to the Kingdom gospel. In just under ten years the whole nation would change, and it wouldn't cost $500 billion dollars to do it.

Even these conservative figures may not be feasible, but

you catch my drift. A little Kingdom leaven could certainly elevate a substantial part of our national loaf. That which starts as the smallest seed would soon grow into the largest tree (Mark 4:30-32). The small beginnings of fiery revival would be fanned into an ardent blaze; one that encompasses and saves most of our nation and the world.

Why Won't Jesus Return until the Kingdom Gospel is Preached in Every Nation? A Partial Gospel Cannot Transform it.

So how does this work, this super prolific fruitfulness? Can you imagine a bowl full of spiritual fruit in each person's heart; delicious morsels so sweet they makes all others nearby crave a taste? The sweetness of love would be like the ripest raspberries, the tranquil tasty melons may resemble peace and the delectable tangy pineapples taste like effervescent joy. To mix metaphors, such a bowl of spiritual fruit in each of God's people would send a fragrant spiritual bouquet into the atmosphere as the sweet savor of Christ permeates the entire environment and blesses all who get close to it.

Jesus told us how this can happen. He said the Kingdom of Heaven is like seed which, when planted in good ground, can't help but reproduce (Mark 4:26-28). Of course, to be that effective, the seed must first die (John 12:24). You knew there was a catch; a price to be paid far greater than our modest spiritual purse wants to bear. Yet this is precisely where some of the greatest blessings of His Kingdom become ours. Jesus said ***"Unless a seed goes***

into the ground and dies it abides alone, but if it dies it bears much fruit" (John 12:24). At first we may think, 'that's it, there's the rub.' Yet upon closer examination, this very verse contains within it the remarkable secret to ending our loneliness. Without this death to self, we remain alone, alienated, separated from all others; an unhappy human island of emptiness, depression and despair. Christians who disdain spiritual fruit bearing are as self-centered and egocentric as people who refuse to have children or marry because they don't want the cost, mess and inconvenience. Sadly, they also miss the incredible blessing that only spiritual children and grandchildren can bring into their lives.

Fortunately, Jesus' very life points the way out of this dilemma. As we explore how he resolved his own agonizing personal conflict with a painful cruel death, we learn what we must do as well. Once and for all, in Gethsemane, He swallowed the only medicine that can save our mortal soul from the relentless corruption of selfishness. "Never the less, not my will but thine," He prayed. In so doing, he ingested the bitterest pill in all of human history, and the only one capable of freeing us all from the fatal dis-ease of selfishness. He simply consented to die for us.

Yet this was a wise and poignant choice; one pregnant with hope for all mankind, because He too had a self interest. ***"For the joy set before Him He endured the cross," (Hebrews 12:2)***; joy and supreme fruitfulness. Just as the seed of His incomparable life went into the ground and died, ***He bore more fruit than any other human in***

history. Today over two billion people self identify as Christians, far more than any other religion in the world. To say He became the first born among many brethren (Romans 8:29) is a massive understatement.

Jesus flung open heaven's gate, forever ending God the Father's loneliness as well as our own. But here's the best news: because He forever faced down the terrifying sting of death (I Corinthians 15:55-6), we can too. Each time we reluctantly face death to our self, all we must do is yield to Him, the Christ within, and He will do the same for us. Thus the incomparable power of His resurrection becomes ours whenever we choose to tap into it. And it will bring us the self- same joy it brought Him. Perhaps this is a big part of what is meant by "Christ in you the hope of glory" (Romans 5:2).

Ironically, I suspect that the greatest resistance to this scriptural strategy of every person making disciples won't come from the unchurched but from religious people. Their belief systems and ecclesiastical power bases could be threatened just as they were when Jesus challenged the Pharisees.

Again. if we want God to grant our every prayer request,we must abide in Him and His Word.

If we want to receive the awesome promises of God's Kingdom, we must be prepared to do the King's business. First and foremost that means becoming spiritually fruitful. Healthy fruit trees produce fruit naturally; it's what they're created to do. Or, as Jesus said, when we abide in the Vine, we can't help but generate lasting fruit (John 15:16). This is the hallmark of a true disciple. How do we abide in Him? Even that is good news. We do it by living in His love (verses 1-15), and that just may be the very best news of all!

> *"By this is my Father glorified, that you bear much fruit; so you will be my disciples." But even in this God wasn't thinking of what He got from it! "These things I have spoken to you that My joy may remain in you and your joy may be full." – John 15:8, 11.*

WIFM? It's in our own best interests to abide in Him. Only then can we fully experience His fullness of joy every day.

> *"Go therefore and make disciples of all the nations, baptizing them in the name of the Father and of the Son and of the Holy Spirit, teaching them to observe all things I have commanded you; and lo, I am with you always, even to the end of the age.' Amen." – Matthew 28:19-20*

DISCUSSION QUESTIONS:

How do you define fruitfulness?

____

____

____

____

____

____

Does this differ from how Jesus defined it? If so, how?

____

____

____

____

____

____

What would keep you from a more fruitful life as He defined it?

____

____

____

____

____

____

CHAPTER SEVEN

KEY THREE: THE SECRET TO SATISFACTION

"Blessed are those who hunger and thirst for righteousness for they shall be filled." – Matthew 5:6

"If you know that He is righteous, you know that everyone who practices righteousness is born of Him." – I John 2:29

"He who sows righteousness gets a true reward" - (Proverbs 11:18).

WHO DOESN'T WANT A FULFILLING LIFE? When I was in a rock band the Rolling Stone's "Satisfaction" was a huge hit. Just preceding the social upheaval of the late 60's, the lyrical refrain of "I can't get no satisfaction," struck a chord with an entire generation that would soon undergo a cultural revolution more traumatic than any our nation ever faced. We knew that money, possessions, starched white shirts and the status quo wouldn't fulfill us and we desperately longed to fill our inner emptiness. But what would do that? For most, the question never got resolved.

Sadly, for lack of a better answer, the vast majority of baby boomers who yearned for satisfaction have long since reverted back to materialistic pursuits. For many, it's still as if 'he who dies with the most toys wins.'

Today's Church shows similar signs of deep discontent. Some sort of "neo reformation" is brewing. Christian pollster George Barna says this frustration "is about an explosion of spiritual energy and activity". He calls it the Revolution (Barna, George, *Revolution*, p. viii). In his provocative book he mentions various indexes that reveal the superficiality and sinfulness of many Churchgoers today. He asks, "Why are most churched Christians so spiritually immature and desperate?" (IBID, p. 30). I would maintain that they wouldn't be nearly as troubled if they truly understood one of Jesus' beatitudes: *"Blessed are those who hunger and thirst for righteousness for they ('their emptiness') shall be filled."* Beatitude means supreme blessedness or bliss. True righteousness is an essential ingredient in God's Kingdom and a major key to the abundant life Jesus came to give us. It truly fuels our fulfillment at the deepest level of our being.

If the social discontent in the 60's led to a radical shift in our moral paradigm and if the Church is similarly dissatisfied today, what's going on spiritually? More importantly, what does it forebode? If we know that money, romance, fun, a great career and religion won't make us happy, what will?

Devout Christ followers must search the scriptures to understand what they say will satisfy us. Only then can we find a dependable answer. So let's examine what Jesus meant when He said the blessing of hungering and thirsting for righteousness will ultimately fill us up.

Righteousness is one of the three major benefits that characterize God's Kingdom. It's also the only other thing besides His Kingdom that we're to seek above everything else (Matthew 6:33-4). Why? We're told that if we seek first His Kingdom and righteousness we'll receive everything else we need. And by righteousness, this doesn't mean persnickety club house rules which appear godly but do little to address our real problems (Colossians 2:20-23). Righteousness goes far beyond our sins of commission to include our manifold sins of omission.

Righteousness is more than the absence of wrongishness. Authentic Christianity is less about what we do wrong and more about what we do right. Even more than that, as we've seen, the very definition of God's Kingdom is "righteousness, peace and joy in the Holy Spirit" (Romans 14:17). Righteousness is the secret sacred key that can unlock that ever elusive fulfillment for which we all yearn (Matthew 5:6). It's a major component of the riches we find in the buried treasure He offers us. It is part of the field we must buy to procure that hidden Kingdom treasure (Matthew 13:44-5). Without it, we still won't "get no satisfaction."

Barna points out that this deep discontentment drives most Christians to struggle just like their secular neighbors and often fail in exactly the same ways. This includes divorce, drug usage (prescriptions as well as illicit), comfort food, alcohol abuse, sexual immorality, work addiction and relationship problems. This explains why so many people, disenchanted with the organized church, seek a radical change in American Christianity. Reporting on this burgeoning disillusionment, Barna said this discontentment exists, not because people don't want Jesus, but because they want more of Him than they can find in existing churches with a partial gospel!

The Revolutionary Neo-Reformation

Amazingly, it is estimated that hundreds of thousands of people leave organized churches every year, but most don't stop worshiping, pursuing Christian fellowship or Bible study. Many form home churches and small fellowship groups where they can develop greater intimacy with God and one another. Weary of dogmatic Bible studies, they yearn for an authentic biblical lifestyles. They long to be more like Jesus and they know that rehashed Christian doctrine won't help them achieve that. The very essence of eternal life isn't just about going to heaven when we die. ***Eternal life is defined as "knowing God and Jesus whom He has sent" (John 17:3).*** And that begins in this life.

It is one thing to talk about knowing God, quite another to really do so. A relationship with the Living God isn't all sweetness and light. In fact, "We must through many tribulations enter the kingdom of God" (John 14:22).

That's because, as Bible teacher Bob Mumford used to say, "When you meet God you meet the first Person in your life you can never manipulate."

Erwin McManus pastors a thriving nOn denominational (former Southern Baptist) mega church in Los Angeles, but it's not your daddy's Baptist Church. Sunday nights it met in a downtown LA nightclub surrounded by 50 foot Mayan statues, strobe lights and electronic music. It now meets on multiple campuses. In his book, The Barbarian Way, he challenges us and his congregation – average age 24 – to embrace primitive Christianity – the true, gritty, gutsy religion of Jesus and the Apostles. He bemoans the fact that Christianity moved from a 'tribe of renegades to a religion of conformists'. He says, "Those who choose to follow Jesus become partners in an insurrection. To claim we believe is simply not enough. The call of Jesus is one that demands action" (McManus, Irwin, *The Barbarian Way*, p. 5).

But spiritual dissatisfaction isn't the sole concern of Gen-Xers and Gen-Zs. It's seeping into mainstream churches. As mentioned, the hot thing on some seminary campuses is "Spiritual Formation" to form the life of Christ into believers. Sadly, today's church is so far removed from that worthy goal that a movement had to spring up to fill the void.

A spiritual formation alliance to which I once belonged defines their goals this way: "The people of God have discovered, in their spiritual growth journey, a clear awareness of the abiding presence and profound love of God in all circumstances of their daily lives. They are so on fire with the love of God that love for neighbor near and far flows naturally to those that don't know that love and to those that need its touch. These spiritually growing followers of Jesus have a passion to live out the invitations of the Gospel in a secular world by compassionately embodying a life of love as seen in Jesus Christ." I believe that's the primary essence of realized righteousness.

If we truly follow the Bible, this should be normal Christian life. Someone said the Church was designed to be a lifeguard station but as it became successful, it stopped rescuing drowning people and morphed into an exclusive beach club. Sadly, today's church is too often little more than a religious social club filled with nice, innocuous people.

Incredibly, the word nice is not used in the Bible one time!

Perhaps this echoes the warning Dietrich Bonhoeffer before he sacrificed his life to expose the Nazis. He said, *"The sin of respectable people reveals itself in the flight from responsibility."* Our worst flight from responsibility is not taking the great commission seriously. All Christians are commanded to both be disciples and make disciples (Matthew 28:18-20). However, Barna says, "In a typical week, only on in four believers will allocate some time to serving other people" (IBID, *Revolution*, p. 34).

Consider these symptoms: habitual self-destructive sins, spiritual lethargy (lukewarmness), the destruction of the nuclear family and people leaving Churches in droves.

How did our 'faith' become so unfaithful? Why do so many cry for insurrection, a neo-reformation, a revolution or the risky Barbarian Way? Is it possible that people just want to return to the original message of primitive Christianity, the Kingdom gospel that Jesus taught and embodied? ***Are we simply longing for the genuine good news that God's Kingdom can truly magnanimously manifest on earth as it is in heaven?***

To understand how we got here we must reconsider the primitive roots of the Protestant Reformation. Medieval monk Martin Luther grew frustrated and weary from all the good works the Church required in order to get to heaven. He traveled to Rome thinking he'd be rejuvenated by the wholesome spiritual atmosphere of the "seat of the Church". Instead he was scandalized by its abject corruption and decay. To fund the Pope's aggressive building programs (I call it an edifice complex), wealthy Church members were sold 'indulgences'. These huge donations to the Churches' coffers supposedly bought them a way out of centuries of purgatory – a fiery way station on the path to heaven that Catholics believe purges people of their sins. Churchgoers were also taught rituals of fasting and self-mortification to crucify their flesh and force it into submission to God.

Luther immediately saw through the mixed motivations of the Church hierarchy. He knew the abject futility of his own efforts to become holy enough to earn his way into heaven. After meticulously attempting to beat his own body into submission, Luther finally acknowledged that spiritual or physical self-flagellation didn't work and never would. In desperation, he turned to the scriptures. When he read, "The just shall live by faith" (Romans 1:17), he fully relinquished his life to the Lord and instantly experienced an intimate personal relationship with the risen Christ.

Understandably, Luther angrily reacted to the 'works righteousness' of Catholicism that had failed him so miserably. In an overreaction to it he developed his doctrine of ***sola faith*** – justification by faith alone. In response to the excesses of his day, he so adamantly insisted on his creed of salvation by faith alone that he tried cut the book of James from his Bible and throw it into the Elbe River. He had to exclude James from his canon because it clearly teaches that ***faith alone cannot save us, but must be united with good deeds*** (James 2:14-26).

Luther swung the pendulum too far in the other direction. His extreme response to medieval Catholicism plagues the Church to this day, robbing us of the exceedingly great blessings of realized righteousness. It keeps us shackled to the mediocrity of living a Sunday only version of what Francis Schaeffer called 'second story religion' – a faith divorced from practical earth bound relevance in our daily lives on Monday through Saturday. Consequently, with its over emphasis on the afterlife, fundamentalists are perceived as being *too heavenly minded to be any earthly good.*

As Luther reacted to the false religion of his day, we must also address the excesses and omissions of today's Church if there is to be a genuine neo-reformation. In fact, what we truly need is what I call 'Vive-al'. You can't revive something that's never been alive, and sadly, many Christians who believe they are saved and heaven bound have never been born again. Therefore they don't really have the life of Christ in them to be revived. Don't think I'm just talking about liberal churches. Many of these spiritual stillborns faithfully attend tepid doctrinally correct evangelical churches.

Whenever I get a chance to discuss this with mega church pastors I ask them one of my rude questions: what percent of their seemingly thriving church would they say are truly born again disciples of Jesus Christ. They usually look down sadly before answering, as if I'd exposed some dreadful spiritual family secret. Even in churches that boast of thousands of people going through their doors each week, the consensus of my unscientific straw poll concludes that only about 15% are truly born again! And unless one is born again he can't even see God's kingdom so he sure won't know how to enter it (John 3:3-5). *This is perhaps the greatest reason why Jesus' mission included opening the eyes of the spiritually and physically blind (Luke 4:18-19).*

What's the Fatal Flaw in Fundamentalism?

If you're wondering if you need to be vived rather than revived, ask yourself this: are you born again? Was your decision for Christ accompanied by a profound life-changing encounter with the Holy Spirit that opened your inner eyes to Kingdom reality? If you can't say absolutely yes, then you probably haven't been reborn. Fortunately the solution is simple. If you seek God with your whole heart you will find Him (Jeremiah 29:13). And when you find Him, your entire life as well as you're the eyes of your heart will dramatically open.

How can so many decent Bible believing Christians miss these greatest essentials? In contrast to lukewarm innocuous niceness, Jesus didn't mince words. ***He said that God's Kingdom suffers violence and violent men seize it by force (Mathew 11:12).***

The Moronic Menace of Modernism

To understand how we got here we also must consider Modernism's assault on Christianity in the late 19th and early 20th centuries. As the theory of evolution gained respectability and technology progressed in many ways, people began to believe that science had more reasonable answers to life than God did. As segregation between whites and blacks became an issue, liberal churches turned away from the Bible in their desperation to make church meaningful for social justice warriors. In reaction, Bible believing Christians sought to staunch the spiritual bleeding. They did so by determining the essential 'fundamental' doctrines which a person must believe to be a true Christian.

As they codified their spiritual litmus test, they included things like the inerrancy of scripture, the virgin birth, the deity of Christ and other true scriptural tenets. There's no problem with these fundamentals. *The trouble this distilled 'faith' down to intellectual ascent to correct dogma.*

Fundamental beliefs became the foundation for church membership and the determining factor for authentic faith. "Believe on the Lord Jesus Christ and you shall be saved" got watered down to "Do you believe Jesus is God, and He was raised from the dead?" Those who said yes were numbered amongst the redeemed; those who didn't were doomed, no matter how they lived their lives in service to mankind. ***There was no understanding of the fact that true biblical faith means total obedient trust.***

Someone said for every complicated problem there's a simple solution that's wrong. This was a classic case in point. All other biblical passages that addressed the necessity of scriptural faithfulness went by the wayside in an attempt to find an easy way to determine if someone was going to heaven.

The Relevant Role of Revivalism

Revivalism gained a head of steam in the wake of Fundamentalism's ascendancy. In 1871, Dwight Moody, one of the early revivalists, led evangelistic meetings in Chicago on the morning of the terrible fire. He encouraged people to go home and think about whether or not they really wanted Jesus to be their Lord. Later the fires savaged the city and thousands died. Believing that many who had attended his morning message perished without saving faith, Moody vowed to never again preach the 'gospel' without offering people an opportunity to immediately get right with God. That became the standard for most other evangelists and churches that followed.

In an attempt to help people make instant conversions, revivalist counselors were trained to ask inquirers if they believed Jesus rose from the dead. If they did, they were given scriptures to assure them they were eternally saved, regardless of whether they were born again or Spirit filled. Supposedly this was to make sure that people's faith was established on a solid biblical foundation and not emotions. This quickly became the standard way to evangelize. The problem is that 'text without context is pretext'. One scripture alone is thoroughly inadequate to explain something as profoundly important as one's eternal destiny.

In these revivals, it looked like lots of great things were happening and people were getting saved by the droves. Evangelistic super stars blew into town and got hundreds if not thousands of notches on their gospel belts. But the actual number of people who were truly transformed by such decisions was minuscule compared to the numbers quoted by the evangelists. In seminary we often joked that anyone stretching the truth was 'speaking evangelistically.'

For most revivalists, discipleship became optional if it were even mentioned at all. When I was a pastor, I became so disgruntled with this approach that I refuse to give an alter call unless I know someone will see that those who respond are properly discipled.

In a zealous fervor to take the gospel to the world, churches recruited fundamentalist missionaries and deployed them to foreign lands while the guy in the pew was tapped to support them financially. He believed that this was his way of participating in the Great Commission. However, it became the great Omission, because Jesus' Great Omission was actually given to every person in the pew. Not only was he or she never encouraged to make disciples, now they didn't even have to be one. Someone else to do it all for them. ***As Jesus said, the mark of a true disciple is that he or she bears lasting fruit (John 15:16).*** *Sadly*, hardly anyone trains their people to make organic disciples today.

It's said that Billy Graham's greatest regret is that only two percent of his converts stayed converted. They call it the Graham Effect. That should haunt him. Both his message and the methods of his mass crusades were unbiblical. His perpetual judgmental emphasis on hell and damnation turned more people off than on. What's worse, most who went forward to receive Christ were simplistically encouraged to believe that they had gotten their ticket punched to heaven just by saying the sinner's prayer. The vast majority of these 'converts' soon fell away. *Most of the rest became religious instead of righteous.* Just as in Jesus' parable of the sower, they had no firm root in themselves (Matthew 13:21).

Fodder for the Great Falling Away

Many of these spiritually stillborn 'believers' became the greatest enemies of true Christianity. At the Christian coffee houses I ran in the mid 1970's, the people whose hearts were most hardened against the Bible were those who said, "Oh yeah, I tried that already. It didn't do anything for me." If you look at the early writings of Vladimir Lenin, the man who birthed the Bolshevik revolution that subjugated and murdered untold millions of Russians and Europeans in the name of atheism, you would never imagine he was once a fiery evangelist. He turned against his shallow faith and became one of Christ's greatest enemies. Near the end of his life, after witnessing the abject failure of atheistic Communism, he said the world would have been better off with ten Jesus of Nazareth's than tens thousand Bolsheviks. This is especially poignant when we consider that the word Christian originally meant 'little Christ.'

If the gospel of the Kingdom is to be preached to the entire world it must start with us. The gospel of 'easy believism' has already done way too much to turn off a few generations. If we don't hurry and get it right, America will become as spiritually moribund as Europe and no amount of culture wars will turn things around.

That's why I say forget about revival, let's go for Vive-al. Let's find ways to advance scriptural discipleship and help those who think they are saved discover the joys of a real encounter with the living God and His risen Christ. As Jack Heyford once said, "Nothing changes until hearts change" (not just minds).

Righteousness must naturally follow in the wake of this 'Vive-al'. Without it, when Jesus returns, He won't find bona fide biblical faithfulness (Cf. Luke 18:8). John warns us not to be deceived: we must be righteous as Jesus was

(I John 3:7). And this is not a boring laborious chore. It's why theologian and novelist Frederick Beuchner's comment is so poignant. He said God's purpose is where your great passion meets the world's deep needs. Your unique desire to care for others is the secret key to your own fulfillment. It's what you were born to do.

Why God's Perfect Will?

Once you insist on doing God's perfect will instead of settling for His permissive will, it's essential that you answer this provocative question: what is your personal mission statement. Mine is to equip the Church to heal and disciple the nations. My greatest pleasure emerges when I help people intimately connect with God and discover His deep transformational healing (Cf. Jeremiah 30). They inevitably experience God's trustworthy love, tranquility and joy. We need not fear His perfect will. The great good news embodied within realized righteousness is that we get to explore our fondest dreams and do what we truly want to do with our life. Somewhere in our deeply buried dreams we can encounter God's impeccable plan for us. Since He knew us before we were in our mother's womb (Jeremiah 1:5), He expressly created us to do those very things.

When Jesus spoke of the conditions for inheriting God's Kingdom, He shared some remarkable parables. One compares the Second Coming of Jesus to the Bride Groom returning for His pristine bride (Revelations 21:2). He commended the ten virgins who were prepared when the bridegroom came. These virgins who were immediately admitted to the eternal wedding banquet had enough oil for their lamps, referring to the Holy Spirit keeping the lamp of their life shining brightly. The ten other excluded virgins had no oil, and were left to languish in the outer darkness(cf.Matthew 25).

What exactly does that mean? The best explanation I ever heard for outer darkness came from a pastor who's dad was a Hollywood star. He had been raised with enough money to buy elegant clothes and expensive sports cars and to party hardy and get almost any young woman he wanted. One day, he went all alone to a desert park to do drugs. Suddenly he collapsed to the ground. Instead of going straight to heaven or hell, everything instantly went black. He found himself ethereally floating in a dark cold space with no light, noise, or any other people. He soon realized he could be in that harsh black solitary state forever. He had heard about Jesus but was sure that being a Christian meant he had to give up having fun and everything he enjoyed. He cried out to Buddha. No answer. Same with Zoroaster, various Hindu deities and any other god force he could remember but nothing changed. After untold minutes in that pitch-dark, terrifying lonely space he finally shouted into the relentless silence, "Jesus help me!I'll do anything you say! Save me! I give you my life!" He immediately found himself alive and lying on the hot desert floor. As he got up, he noticed a bright angelic being hovering over him smiling. He brushed himself off and started walking back to where he came from. A voice inside his head whispered,

"You just overdosed! That wasn't Jesus. You had a bad dream. It's all an illusion!" He wanted to believe that so he did. He smiled and told himself he could return to his old life after all. Over the next couple of weeks, people he didn't even know walked up to him and said, "God told me to tell you it wasn't an illusion." He looked at each one like they were crazy and walked away. But after the third or fourth time, he prayed, "Okay Jesus I believe you!" And he surrendered his life back to the Lord. He ended up using his music skills to become a worship leader and Christian pastor during the early days of the Jesus Movement. When I met him, he had happily served the Lord for over 50 years.

In the same chapter Jesus shared the parable of the separation of the sheep and the goats, again referring to God's judgment (cf. Matthew 25). But the redeemed sheep weren't people who passed some sort of 'spiritual SAT exam', to coin John Eldredge's brilliant metaphor. They were those who fed the hungry, clothed the naked, welcomed the stranger, and visited the sick and imprisoned. They alone had true religion (cf. Matthew 25), while those who had false religion faced a sad pitiful destiny.

Did you know that religion is only mentioned three times in the entire Bible and only one passage spoke of it in somewhat positive terms. It's where James told us that undefiled religion is to "to visit orphans and widows in their trouble and to keep oneself unspotted from the world" (James 1:27).

The True Body of Christ has Eyes, Ears, Hands and Feet, not just a Mouth.

Those qualities that comprise true religion and manifest it visibly are the essence of realized righteousness. A statue of Jesus in Europe was hit by bombs that took off the just hands of Jesus. When they considered whether to tear it down or rebuild it they decided instead to put this noticed chiseled into stone in front of it: ***Jesus has no other hands but yours.***

So what is realized righteousness? As we'll see, it's quite different from holiness and far more than the absence of wrongishness. In fact, all the stress on 'holiness' in fundamentalist churches, religious radio, contemporary worship and guilt based preaching only makes things worse. As the Apostle Paul said, pseudo holiness has the show of religion, but denies its substance (Colossians 2:20-23). I'd say it majors in minors and doesn't even minor in God's mandated majors. Where the Spirit of the Lord is there is liberty (II Corinthians 3:17); where religious spirits prevail, only bondage. Biblical preaching and worship should always be generously seasoned with grace (Ephesians 4:29).

John Wesley was best known for his doctrine of perfection; that we could be perfected in this life. Sadly much pseudo holiness sprung from that teaching and defined holiness very differently from the way Wesley did. He understood that the word for true holiness means **separate**, and it's not only separation from evil but separation of our life ***to God to do good. Wesley biblically***

defined holiness as perfect love, being perfect as our heavenly Father is who made rain to fall and sun to rise on the just and the unjust. Conversely, the religious hoop jumping my spiritual father described as, 'Do not drink, do not chew, do not go with girls who do,' leads worse than nowhere. Why? It binds people to the very sins they seek to avoid. Ironically, false legalism is why the Church is so unholy. The law of sin and death starts the downward death spiral that plunges people towards dissipation and destruction. (Read Romans chapters six through eight very carefully.)

So what is realized righteousness? I believe it's the positive expression of God's love in response to human need. The reason it's so fulfilling is because, in the immortal words of Saint Francis: "It is in giving that we receive".

Someone once said "We must ***tangibilitate*** God: make him palpably evident by sharing His love. That's the key to experiencing deep lasting joy and the abiding Presence of God's delicious love (Cf. John 15:10-11). It keeps the lamps of our lives filled with God's oil. We don't burn out from burning the wick instead of the oil; we have enough fuel in our spiritual tanks to get us to the wedding feast. This describes the exuberant energy that true righteousness produces in us. Our light shines because our life shines, gloriously radiating His perfect love to the world around us. A famous atheist observed the response of thousands of Christians to the Hurricane Katrina relief efforts and noted that it was almost enough to make him believe in Jesus. ***After all, what school, college or hospital was ever***

started by an atheist?

No wonder righteousness is one of three key components in kingdom reality (Romans 14:17). No wonder it alone can deliver on the promise to fulfill us (Matthew 5:3). This defines the essential neo-reformation we actually need, not just some vacuous revolution or nondescript spiritual formation. The transformation that the Church truly needs will only come once righteousness is embraced and assumes its prominent role in our life and theology. I had a Seminary professor who said *"The world has a right to look at the Church and see love. When it doesn't see love, it has a right to say that the Church doesn't exist."* He was so right. Living Love produces spiritual within each Christ follower fruit, and spiritual reproduction and fullness of joy. ***No wonder it's the key to answered prayer!***

But it goes far deeper than that. In Jesus's ultimate parabolic metaphor for eternal bliss and agony, when He shockingly described the last judgment as the separation of goats from sheep (Cf. Matthew 25:31-46), the righteous sheep who will blissfully inherit God's forever Kingdom gave food and drink to the hungry and thirsty, clothed the naked, visited the imprisoned and sheltered the homeless. These very acts were a natural part of their spiritual DNA; they truly lived like the God who is the epitome of compassionate sacrificial love. They were authentic children of the King of kings. The evil religious goats did none of these things. Their eternal lot? The everlasting fire and torment which God prepared for "the adversary and his (fallen) angels." Harsh? Take it up with Jesus.

Hypocritical religious people demanded His death in the first century. Their judgmental self-righteous lifestyle still betrays Him today.

> *"Unless your righteousness exceeds that of the scribes and Pharisees, you will by no means enter the kingdom of heaven" (Matthew 5:20).*

> *"What does it profit, my brethren, if someone says he has faith but does not have works? Can faith save him? Faith by itself, if it does not have works, is dead" (James 2:14, 17).*

> *"Be careful to maintain good works. These things are good and profitable to men.... Let our people also learn to maintain good works, to meet urgent needs, that they not be unfruitful." - (Titus 3:8b, 14).*

> *"What the wicked fears will come upon him, And the desire of the righteous will be granted" (Proverbs. 10:24).*

> *"Little children, let no one deceive you; the one who practices righteousness is righteous, just as He is righteous; the one who practices sin is of the devil; for the devil has sinned from the beginning. The Son of God appeared for this purpose, that He might destroy the works of the devil. No one who is born of God practices sin, because His seed abides in him; and he cannot sin, because he is born of God. By this the children of God and the children of the devil are obvious: anyone who does not practice righteousness is not of God, nor one who does not love his brother" - (I John 3:7-10).*

DISCUSSION QUESTIONS

In your own words, explain how realized righteousness leads to personal satisfaction and fulfillment?

What do you do in your life that would fit Jesus' definition of righteousness?

How could your personal passion help meet the world's great needs?

CHAPTER EIGHT

KEY FOUR: PROMISES OF PERFECT PEACE

"Blessed are the peacemakers, for they shall be called sons of God." – Matthew 5:9

"The peace of God, that passes all understanding, will guard your hearts and minds through Christ Jesus." – Philippians 4:7

"Blessed is a person who finds wisdom, and one who obtains understanding. ... Her ways are pleasant ways, And all her paths are peace. She is a tree of life to those who take hold of her, and happy are those who hold on to her." - Proverbs 3:13, 17-18

SHALOM, PERSONAL PEACE, THE PRECIOUS PROMISE of the profoundest of all blessings. When I became a Christian during the Viet Nam war I was shocked to discover that the Bible talks more about peace than speakers at an anti-war rally. Jesus is the Prince of Peace

(Isaiah 9:6) and *sheikh* of *shalom* (the Hebrew word for peace). Those who live in Him have peace (Romans 5:1). He is our peace (Ephesians 2:14). This reminds me of a bumper sticker from the Jesus movement: ***"No Christ, no peace. Know Christ, know peace."***

Peace is one of the delicious fruits of God's indwelling Spirit (Galatians 5:22). Jesus offers us a type of tranquility that transcends any peace we can ever find in this world (Phil. 4:7). Sadly, a large percentage who consider themselves Christians don't experience such peace. That's why so many need antidepressants. Most who have said the sinner's prayer were never encouraged to surrender their lives to Christ's lordship. Many have neither been born again nor filled their inner emptiness with the benevolent presence of the Holy Spirit. That's why so many have no experiential knowledge of the deep personal peace that He alone can provide. As I sought the best title for my transformational healing workbook, I would ask groups of people if anyone wanted *Peace Without Prozac*. When almost everyone asked where they could get it now, I knew I'd found the right title.

The peace which Christ gives us is far more comprehensive than anything we can find anywhere else. That's precisely why Shalom is the universal blessing of Jews. The best description I've seen of God's peace was penned by William Barclay. He says scriptural peace is never just a negative state, the absence of trouble or even of war. It means everything that leads to our highest good, the presence of all good things; not just freedom from bad things but also enjoyment of all good (Barclay, William,

The Gospel of Matthew, Volume I, pg. 108).

The New Bible Dictionary expands this definition to include "completeness, soundness, harmony, concord, material prosperity and well-being" (p. 956). It tells us that the Messianic hope was for an age of such comprehensive peace (Isaiah 2:2-4, 11:1-9, Haggai 2:7-9). Jesus delivered that peace, but not in the governmental sense that the first century Jews hoped. His peace is personal, not political. By making the Holy Spirit accessible to all, it can dwell within whomever yields their life to God (John 1:12, Romans 5:5).

The prophet Jeremiah lamented that religious leaders promised peace but never delivered it (Jeremiah 6:14, 8:11, 15). The reason? They only healed the wounds of God's people superficially (Jeremiah 6:14, 8:11). Hence there was no balm in Gilead, no effective physician, no complete recovery for God's chosen people (Jeremiah 8:22).

Jeremiah predicted that because the sins of God's people were destroying them they would endure cruel captivity at the hands of their enemies. The people were so incensed that Jeremiah would condemn God's people like that they beat him, tortured him and dragged him through manure in a vain attempt to shut him up. Some religious people would like to do that today at any indication that the Holy Spirit is necessary or hasn't been fully experienced. When I was in seminary, a man wrote a book entitled *Let's Stop Fighting Over the Holy Spirit*. Its message has yet to be embraced by many Christians. Though the Bible clearly teaches that Jesus is the same yesterday, today and forever, some famous televangelists rail against any who suggest that God's Spirit does miracles today. Some even call charismatics demonic. If this isn't the unforgivable sin of blasphemy of the Holy Spirit I don't know what is.

There's truly nothing new under the sun (Ecclesiastes 1:9). Like the frozen chosen in ancient Israel, those who consider themselves His elect today are often similarly enraged at the thought that God's people need healing and suffer if they don't acquire it. Yet the Churches' bondage to stubborn addictions plague many religious Christians if not all. The secular world is scandalized by revelations that Christians' problems with immorality, food and substance abuse, divorce and the numerous moral plagues of our modern age parallel those of our unchristian neighbors. King David, Solomon, the Apostle Paul and Abraham would not be welcome in many such hyper religious churches today.

Finally, Jeremiah foretold a time when God would heal the painful wounds of His people (See Jeremiah chapter 30). God said He would do for us what no medicine could (verse 13). When He did that, amazing blessings would flow into His people and manifest His glory to the entire world (Verses 18-22). We would not understand all this until the latter days (verse 24). This is the very healing that God blessed me to discover when I asked Him where the healing I saw was mentioned in the Bible. It's the fulfillment of Jeremiah 30 and the biblical foundation for my book *Peace Without Prozac*. Jesus the Christ said He came to fulfill these wondrous promises for us (Luke 4:18-19) that Jeremiah said we'd understand in the latter day.

So What Exactly Does Jesus' Name Mean?

We know that biblical names are important and that Jesus is the name above all names, but few know what His name actually means. Jesus' name is pregnant with the incredible promises which Jeremiah made and which were foreshadowed throughout the entire Old Testament. As I said in *Peace Without Prozac* , Jesus is Yeshua, our New Testament Joshua who will lead us into the Promised land of God's incredible Kingdom by saving us from both the power and the penalty of our sins (Matthew 1:21). But like Joshua of Old, He would first have to conquer vicious adversaries who inhabited the land.

Since God's Kingdom is within us, the land He must subdue is the human heart. The ferocious adversaries he must decimate live within us all. This is why Jesus warned us that the things that defile us come from within, out of our own heart (Matthew 15:11). As William Barclay says, "Every man is a walking civil war" (IBID, p. 108).

Fortunately, the very name of Christ tells us how He will help us win the war against our inner enemies. Jesus is our true Messiah; the One anointed to heal our brokenness, release us from our woundedness, and free us from our enslavement to sin so we can fully and powerfully serve the Living God. When He does this, our spiritual blindness will be cured, our personal poverty reversed, and the ultimate year of Jubilee proclaimed, releasing us forever from our indentured servitude to sin. In pointing to the coming Messiah, this was all predicted by Isaiah (cf. Isaiah 61) and fulfilled by Jesus. He announced this to be fundamental to His mission statement in his inaugural address at his home synagogue (Luke 4:16-19). Sadly, when such promises are offered us today, the Jesus who came to do this for us is sometimes rejected almost as unceremoniously as Jesus was when he first proclaimed it (Verse 28-29).

Only as we allow Him to heal our brokenness, can His peace more freely rule our emotions and grant us the courage to be His disciples. ***Healing is essential to the expansion of God's Kingdom on earth.*** I learned this after I led a Transformational Healing Retreat in Cleveland. The next day, some men invited me to meet with a group that included people from the retreat and others who shared a vision for healing. One man had asked the Lord why their prayers for revival went unanswered in Cleveland. He believed the Lord told him that before revival could come, the Church needed healing. I once led a similar event for a church in Arkansas. On the last day an elderly pastor stood up and said he had prayed for 50 years to see people set free like they were at the Transformational Healing Seminar. The pastor told me that seminar was changing his city. His church was smart enough to start a Sunday evening healing service. His church grew from 300 to 650 in four months. The last time I spoke with him they started two new churches with over 1,500 active members.

Why Healing Must Precede True Revival

It's far easier to love people once our own brokenness is

healed. Mother Theresa encouraged people to "Love until it hurts" (*Sunbeams*, Sun Publishing Company, 1990, p. 108). We can't do that very well when we're wounded and hurting.

As I learned about Transformational Healing I was concerned that it would divert me from my calling to equip the Church for discipling the nations. When I began leading Transformational Healing Seminars in churches, ***I watched in amazement as most of those churches spontaneously doubled in size a year or less.*** Their people left the seminar looking five years younger and became healthy enough to share love, forgiveness and compassion with their neighbors. Friends who saw such a transformation wanted to experience the same change.

The churches that continued using Transformational Healing meetings after I left could not help but grow. ***One pastor told me that people from 40 churches attended those Sunday night meetings and it was changing his entire city!*** People would leave those meetings and seek out people they had wounded years earlier to ask for their forgiveness. Those people in turn were irresistibly drawn to acquire that same healing for themselves. Simone Weil said charity means *"to love human beings insofar as they are nothing. That is, to love them as God does"* (IBID., *Sunbeams*). Only the spiritually healthy dare to love like that. When they do, they more fully experience the holistic shalom that only Jesus Christ offers us.

Some religions like Buddhism offer us peace through detachment from problems and conflict but who does that help? A Buddhist nation never would have stood up to

Hitler. As Christians, we can't ignore the world's pain. Even if we don't perceive any personally, our loved ones do. Jesus gives us peace amidst our encounters with the desperate needs of hurting humanity. A homeless man that I see on my daily walk asked me why I'm so kind and generous. "Is that it?" he asked, pointing to the cross around my neck. I said, "Yes, Jesus is my Best Friend." He told me the sad story of how he became homeless and asked me to pray with him. When I see him now, he said his life is getting better and better. I recently gave him some cash for breakfast. He pulled out a beautiful wrist watch he found while searching through trash. When I tried to give it back he insisted I keep it. Truly this is why the peace of Jesus is unlike anything the world can give us (John 14:27).

When we try to help a world full of broken hurting people heal, we are sometimes stricken by the very hands we're trying to help. I recall what a very wise man said when I shared with him the pain I felt from the unjust attack of a parishioner I was counseling. "Sometimes people act just like obstreperous animals," he said. (I had to look up the word obstreperous.) In biblical love, there's no room for Sartre's "Hell is other people" comment. There is also no room for the selfish religious escapism or New Age beliefs.

When Jesus said "Blessed are the peacemakers" (Matthew 5:9), he was not advocating peace at any price in every political conflict. The Bible says we will have wars until the end of history. Jesus even cautioned His disciples to take a sword with them when He sent them out to preach. But His peace deepens our blissfulness as we help people heal and find Him. It's the incomparable joy we experience when they encounter the profound shalom that permeates us even in the midst of strife and turmoil. Scriptural peacemakers help people find spiritual tranquility which is superior to anything the temporal world offers us. It creates an inner oasis deep within our very souls, even in the midst of chaos, turmoil and trials. The prophet Isaiah said God keeps us in perfect peace when our heart and mind is stayed on Him because we trust in Him (Isaiah 26:3).

The songwriter Horatio Spafford, who wrote the immortal words to the beloved hymn "It is well with my Soul," was intimately acquainted with such perfect peace. The lyrics say:

When peace, like a river, attendeth my way,
When sorrows like sea billows roll;
Whatever my lot, Thou has taught me to say,
It is well, it is well, with my soul.

Those are the lyrics he penned when his ship crossed over the spot where his wife and children drowned after colliding with another ship! Without such a fountain of peace, no one could comprehend such sentiments in the deep dark valley of the shadow of death.

The Apostle Paul offered us a peace that surpasses all human understanding and told us how to get it and keep it (Philippians 4:4-8). He went even further when he said that *Jesus is our peace* (Ephesians 2:14). In a very real sense, Jesus restrained our inner civil war by living a sinless life. Through His excruciating death and incomparable resurrection, He then granted us access to the same Holy Spirit that pacified all self-destructive human instincts. And make no mistake, even He had them. If He hadn't, He wouldn't have been fully human or able to be tempted in all things just as we are. Since He overcame His inner adversaries we can too.

This is not achieved through some sort of instantaneous sanctification from a 'second work of grace', as some would claim. We're all a work in progress. God began a good work in us and He promises to fulfill it until Jesus returns or we die (Philippians 1:6). I can honestly say, I'm not what I should be, I'm not what I'm gonna be, but thank God I'm not what I used to be.

Our Very Existence is a Lifelong Healing Journey

It's a persistent, progressive unparalleled growth toward wholeness, deliverance, freedom and healing from our brokenness. His Kingdom continues to expand and increase deep within in us as well as the entire world.

This is very different from the superficial perfectionism of shallow religious teaching. Breaking a few bad habits is never enough. The more we think we can earn God's favor by doing so, the more impossible it is to achieve that goal. God isn't satisfied with arbitrary religious rules. He wants us committed to His perfect love; love that can feel affection for our surly neighbors, our defiant loved one, and yes, even our cruelest adversaries. Often our loved ones become our worst intimate enemies. Some will reside in our own family and church. We may get angry when someone cuts us off on the freeway, but we only hate those who loved us and deeply hurt us the most. Christianity is the only religion that commands us to love our enemies. ***It's the only one that grants us the power to do so.***

So What is True Holiness?

In the original language, the root word for holy is separate. But genuine holiness is not just about separation from evil, it also includes separation to God. And ultimately, all sin is a sin against love, for God is Love. Before they achieve this kind of holiness, every sincere Christian inevitably messes up. A righteous man falls seven times but he gets up eight (Cf. Proverbs 24:16). He will even learn to rejoice in temptation and trials (James 1:2), knowing that they help us become even more Christ like. I've learned far more from the times I've screwed up than I ever would have learned had I done everything right. Such essential lessons impart to us humility, mercy, grace, compassion and even love for fellow sinners. It's purged me of my self-righteous and judgmentalism; well, most of it. The curriculum that dresses us up in the true garment of righteousness can't be taught in a Sunday school class or be totally absorbed from even the best pulpit. It must be fashioned within us in the laboratory of life. Grace and peace are multiplied to us through the true knowledge of God and Jesus (II Peter 1:2); the same God who sent His Son to die for us sinners; the same Son who drank that cup of suffering for the likes of you and me.

This is why a huge part of the gospel of God's Kingdom is the peace which can only come from Christ (Ephesians 6:15). It proceeds as the God of peace sanctifies us, not only in our body but also in our soul and spirit (I Thessalonians 5:23). For then we become perfect as He is perfect (Matthew 5:48): perfect in compassion, perfect in mercy, perfect in God's agape love. How different this is from the sanctimony that so many associate with their experience of *churchianity*; how different, how glorious and how wonderful. That's the kind of good news anyone would embrace.

Going back to Jeremiah 30, I asked the Lord why we would only understand His healing for our wounds in the latter days. I believe He said, "Because there's no such thing as a sin that hurts no one. Sin harms both the sinner and those who are sinned against. And sin will abound more in the latter days than at any other time in history. Healing emotional wounds will be as essential in the last century as healing bodies was in the first."

He led me to write *Peace Without Prozac* to help people self-heal their own brokenness and to train churches, counselors and chaplains to heal others.

> *"The things which you learned and received and heard and saw in me, these do, and the God of peace will be with you." – Philippians 4:9*
>
> *"Peace I leave with you, my peace I give unto you; not as the world gives do I give to you. Let not your heart be troubled, neither let it be afraid" – John 14:27*

"Thou will keep him in perfect peace whose mind is stayed on Thee (Isiah 26:3))."

DISCUSSION QUESTIONS

Would you like more of this perfect peace in your life?

____

____

____

____

____

____

How would it benefit you?

____

____

____

____

____

____

What would you have to do to acquire it?

____

____

____

____

____

____

CHAPTER NINE

KEY FIVE: JOY-FULLNESS FOR SPIRITUAL BLISS

"For the kingdom of God is not meat nor drink but righteousness, peace and joy in the Holy Spirit." - Romans 14:17

"The joy of the Lord is your strength." – Nehemiah 8:10

"These things I have spoken to you that my joy might remain in you, and that your joy be made full." – Jesus, John 15:11

WHAT IS JOY? HOW DO WE TRULY EN-JOY LIFE? God's Word has much to say about that, but I never learned it in Sunday school. As an adolescent, long before I became a Christian, I remember wondering if all of life was lived just for those rare times when we went to amusement parks. As a teenager, I took a girl I wanted to impress to an amusement park. While waiting in line for the roller coaster a bird crapped on my forehead. Maybe even then God was trying to tell me something? I later discovered that the very word amusement says a lot. It literally means *A-MUSE: 'against considering things'*. If we think about life too much we may conclude that it's hardly worth living. So instead of asking that old hamburger commercial question 'where's the beef,' we should probably ask, where's the bliss? Instead of trying to 'grab all the gusto' through beer, we are far better served by grasping the greatest source of true joy in the entire Universe.

I suggest we contrast our little amusements with this brilliant statement by C.S. Lewis: *"We are half-hearted creatures fooling about with drink and sex and ambition when infinite joy is offered us. We are like an ignorant child who wants to go on making mud pies in a slum because he cannot imagine what is meant by the offer of a holiday at the sea. We are far too easily pleased."*

Besides having much to say about righteousness and peace, the Bible also explains how to attain that ever elusive thing called joy. It even teaches us how to get joy in all its fullness and keep it no matter what predicament we find our self in.

In this passage, though joy is the last of the three qualities that defines God's Kingdom it's hardly the least. Sadly, way too few people ever discover the secrets of joy, even in the Church. Someone once said "the pity of the Church is half filled Christians trying to overflow." Perhaps you've been in more arid stale worship services than not and tolerated far too many drab, uninspiring, impractical sermons. I sure have. After all, the Bible says,

"Every man is bullish in his knowledge." Preachers aren't immune to that. I wonder if the slang for bovine excrement came from that verse. (Actually, the word shit is an ancient acronym. When people hauled fertilizer through hot climates in tall ships, they had to make sure it was kept in crates above deck. It got too hot below deck and could start fires. Hence wooden boxes carrying fertilizers where labeled SHIT, which stood for Ship Higher In Transit.)

Moving right along: to help us avoid such un-enjoyable situations, let's examine deep satisfying joy. Only then can we explore how to get more of it and maintain it. Merriam Webster's Dictionary defines joy as "the emotion evoked by well-being, success, or good fortune or by the prospect of possessing what one desires." Synonyms for joy include "happiness, delight, bliss, pleasure, ecstasy and elation." Who wouldn't want more of that? I remember when I first learned that author Joseph Campbell recommends that every person follow their bliss. I saw it as a uniquely wondrous practice that precious few people pursue. Personally, I'm having a blast writing books and films and poetry with the help of my Boss and Best Friend Forever, for whom I work remotely, if you catch my drift.

So where can We Find Joy?

The Bible says joy is found precisely where most who don't truly know Him would least expect it: in God's glorious Presence. He's not some sort of celestial killjoy. I prefer to call Him my Life-joy. Joy is a fruit of His Spirit, an essential ingredient of His very nature. Hence it's an exquisite way to encounter His loving Presence. *And with that joy comes a sense of deep, intimate, heartfelt pleasure (Psalm 16:11).* For King David the Psalmist, God Himself is his joy (Psalm 43:4).

Genuine worship enables us to experience this pleasure, ***for the very God who is Love literally inhabits our praises*** (Psalm 22:3). They bring us into intimate contact with Him at our deepest heartfelt level. Is any emotion more delicious than Love? No wonder Vladimir Lenin, Communist and founder of the Soviet Union, scornfully called it the opiate of the people. It's way better than drugs. With divine joy there are no addictions, high costs, hangovers, arrests or personal devastation and untimely deaths.

We're called to worship God in Spirit and in truth (John 4:23). Sadly, many worship experiences are long on truth and treat the Holy Spirit as an embarrassing afterthought. How many worship services have you seen that are filled with lame lifeless singing? Or others that are little more than a performance? True worship joins mind, emotion and soul in profound adoration of its chief object – the Living God whose very Spirit abides in our praises. Dead worship is little more than mindlessly mouthing words we don't understand or believe. It just can't conjure up this loving divine encounter.

Worship is another fascinating word. It literally means ascribing worth to something or someone. ***We praise God for what He has done, we worship Him for who He is.*** We adore Him for His beautiful, compassionate, loving nature, His astonishing and benevolent wisdom, and extravagant unmerited grace, along with countless other aspects of His sterling personality and character. The word mercy in the Bible is better translated loving kindness. Isn't that a wonderful word? Just think of it: His loving kindness towards you endures forever (cf.Psalm 136).

I couldn't comprehend that kind of love until I had children. Sometimes I don't like what my children do or don't do, but even at their worst I could never wish them ill. I always try to look at them through the eyes of compassion – well, almost always. And as Jesus said, if I being evil, want good things for my children, *how much more does our Heavenly Father who is the essence of goodness want the Holy Spirit for us* (Matthew 7:11). No wonder so many people seek to quench and downplay the beloved Holy Spirit. God's Spirit enables us to become reborn as new people; people capable of fully experiencing the joy of the Lord. And joy is a delightful fruit that flourishes in us on the Spirit's innermost vine (Galatians 5:22). His indwelling Spirit imparts a profound existential encounter with God's affection for us and grants us the delectably palatable sense of His adoring Presence. We might even say, God is in love with us. Perhaps that's why He calls us His bride.

I have a friend who was an agnostic. Before she became a Christian, she asked me what the Holy Spirit was all about. I told her that the Spirit's Presence is like the feeling we get when we hear the Star Spangled Banner or some similar song that moves our emotions deeply. She got that, and when she finally opened her heart to experiencing Him, the Lord met her most powerfully in her prayer life. Nothing could better convince her of His reality and love in ways that intellectual debate or discussions never could. Sometimes God is more real to me than any person I can see, smell or touch with my hands.

I love to en-courage skeptics to simply ask God to show them if He's real. He loves being invited to do that because He knows exactly what every person needs for them to be persuaded. A case in point: at my prompting, another agnostic friend, a former drug dealer, did exactly that. Shortly after praying for God to reveal Himself to him, he accidentally pushed his hand into a car engine he was working on without realizing the quiet motor was running. When a co-worker heard his gloved hand hit the fan blade, he jumped over and pulled him out. My buddy looked at his hand, fully expecting it to be shredded by the razor sharp blades. ***The glove wasn't even creased.*** As he told me about it, he said he felt that an angel protected him. A few nights later he thought about what happened to him and thanked God for His protection before going to sleep. A he closed his eyes, a bright light suddenly startled him. He popped open his eyes only to see his room had filled with angels. He said it was so crowded he could hardly move. Needless to say, he's no longer an agnostic.

In one of His Kingdom parables, Jesus welcomes the faithful servant to enter into the joy of the Lord (Matthew 25:21). Such joy is so great that at times it becomes inexpressible (I Peter 1:8). The Spirit can fill us with joy whenever we need or request it (Romans 15:13). It gives us profound strength in our faith and life whenever that happens (Nehemiah 8:10). This "very present help in time of need" (Psalm 46:1), tangibly reminds us that He will never leave nor forsake us (Hebrews 13:5).

The Holy Spirit is also called the Comforter because it "draws alongside to help" (a key trait of the Holy Spirit). And what wonderful help it offers us. Biblical comfort is far more than an encouraging spiritual hug. A big part of the word comfort is forte, which means strong and powerful.

When Jesus said the Peace He gives us is not as the world gives, He meant that it doesn't depend on tranquil situations. His peace can mysteriously come to us in the midst of chaos and upheaval. I once poured some ice cold vegetables into a pan of very hot coconut oil. Flames shot towards the ceiling. I calmly picked up the pan and carefully walked it outside where the flames instantly stopped. I was awed by my own calm peaceful spirit.

Similarly, for the true believer, the joy of the Lord eclipses any personal unhappiness and even the most dreadful predicaments. The apostle Paul wrote more about joy in the book of Colossians than he did anywhere else. At the time, he was in the most miserable circumstances of his entire life, left to rot alone in a cold, damp, wretched prison cell near the end of his life. Perhaps this is one of the major sources of our strength in the Lord. "Weeping may endure for a night but joy comes in the morning," (Psalm 30:5). It also comes ***through our mourning***. Only then and there do we encounter the greatest comfort (Matthew 5:4).

That's why the hymn "Great is Thy Faithfulness" is so poignant, a vivid testimony to the fact that even in the depth of his greatest grief he encountered the joy of the Lord. We too can know His joy during our most painful moments of despair and suffering. The beatitude *'Blessed are those who mourn for they shall be comforted'* is the very essence of good grief. It grants us calming strength and internal satisfaction that nothing else can.

I know this first hand. As a young Christian, my life was shattered when a woman who I considered the love of my life broke off our engagement. Prior to that, I had little compassion for Christians who got bent out of shape when their heart was romantically broken. I couldn't understand how anyone who had God's love could get so upset over the mere loss of human love. Boy did I find out the hard way. Be careful who you condemn. In a very real way we become what we judge. If you can't learn mercy any other way, God will allow the very thing you judge to happen to you. When she broke up with me, I was so messed up that a few days later I ran into many people at a meeting who I saw every week. They didn't even recognize me; my countenance was that distorted by excruciating emotional pain. At the time, this was the deepest emotional agony I had ever felt as an adult. I was so miserable that for days it was all I could do to not drive my car into every concrete barrier I passed on the highway. Months later I was still distraught to the point that I even questioned God's love. I sincerely wondered if I wanted to serve Him. I became so despondent I had to figure out how to restore my first love for God.

As I thought things through, I realized I had been happy before I met my girlfriend; happy solely in my relationship to Him. Gradually I discovered that He alone was the only dependable source of abiding love and happiness I had ever known or ever would know. I would suffer many losses in life. The grandfather I dearly loved suddenly died when I was ten. Numerous girlfriends wounded me deeply, close friends betrayed me, people who had become Christians in my church seldom even said thank you. Even the best of people would probably let me down, just as I sometimes let others down. I saw that only the Lord's love is unchanging. He alone is the One who promised not only to never leave nor forsake me (Hebrews 13:5), but also to make sure that everything in life would turn out for my highest good. But, as with every promise He makes to us, there was a condition: I had to continue loving Him and yield to His great purpose for my life (Romans 8:28).

True Delight

That was the day the sun rose again in my soul; the day I allowed the Son to return to His rightful place at the center of the constellation of my life. ***Someone said if God is your co-pilot the wrong person is flying the plane!*** I moved over that day and let Him 'take the wheel.' I've never been the same. I finally learned what it means to ***delight in the Lord***. It's simply an acknowledgement that He is the Only One who is absolutely dependable and who will never ever stop loving you; the only One who is continually delighted to be with you. In Him, we can always experience deep, intimate love and even ecstatic pleasure (Psalm 16:11) any time we want to.

Beyond that, it also means that in His Presence we can always experience joy, affection and peace, no matter how bad our external circumstances become. You can read the stories of the Apostle Paul in prison and his contagious joy that led to the conversion of his jailers. Or the indomitable courage of Joan of Arc as she faced the agony of being burned at the stake, or the equanimity of Dietrich Bonhoeffer on the day he was martyred in a Nazi prison, or millions of others who endured the loss of life, loved ones, and possessions. Even facing persecution, torture and painful death for their faith, we see something remarkable. I think of Stephen the first martyr, beatifically gazing up at the angels in heaven awaiting him as an enraged religious mob picked up rocks to stone him (Acts 7-8). No wonder the early church father Tertullian said *"The blood of the martyrs is the seed of the church."* The Spirit that enabled Jesus to unjustly endure agony unlike any that man had ever known and even forgive those who tortured Him; that same very Spirit lived on in all those people. When you yield to His Spirit and welcome it into your innermost being, you too will know a bliss that this world can never bestow. It will help you navigate the inevitable darkness that clouds every life (Ecclesiastes 11:8) and offer you a joy that nothing and no one else ever can.

Delighting in the Lord like this is one of the most wondrous things we can learn in life, for once we delight in Him, He can grant us our heart's desires (Psalm 37:4). God isn't an ego maniac. He's not saying love me and I'll give you stuff. Rather, as we delight in Him, He can grant us our desires just like He wants to do. He then knows we will neither idolize nor be destroyed by them.

God deeply cares about our heart's desires. If he didn't, He would not have told us how to receive them. And He's given us lots of information about that. I'm convinced that God planted the seeds of our desires in our hearts because they reveal our greatest destiny. Our God inspired dreams expose His call on our life; they reveal what He uniquely created each of us to do.

The Perils of Religious Sacrifice

Many of us have heard far too many sermons on sacrifice and self-denial. Years ago, as I was first discovering that God cares about my dreams, I was teaching my course on Sacred Psychology at a church in Georgia. I had recently been given the opportunity to dust off my high school dream of acting, a dream I had been forced to give up 30 years earlier when my family refused to allow me to study drama at NYU. I was excitedly sharing this with my class because I wanted them to see how the Lord also cared about *all their dreams*. One particularly religious man was offended because he felt I was abandoning my higher calling as a pastor to pursue some carnal worldly career in acting and film. He couldn't grasp the possibility that God could use me more in making films that reflect His glory than He could by preaching to even a very large congregation. In the wake of the ensuing controversy, I was unceremoniously released from my position as head of the school's department of counseling.

It's a shame that so few Christians understand how deeply the Lord cares about what we care about. It often drives many people to New Age groups and 'new thought' churches where people have a better grasp on the God who is the very embodiment of Love. Many rigid, dogmatic orthodox churches don't have a clue. I eventually found so much in the Bible about our heart's desire and how to attain it that I developed a course and seminar called ***Sacred Secrets to an Abundant Life***. It's a biblical primer on how to attain your dreams and fulfill your calling and destiny through faith.

An important part of this topic circles back to the issue of joy. Jesus teaches us how His joy remains in us and is made full (read John 15). He also shows us how to get answers to all our prayers. He simply said that if we obey God's commands we will abide in His love, and if we abide in Him and allow His Word to abide in us, whatever we desire will be granted for us. ***Jesus told us that so that our joy would remain in us and be made full.*** Doesn't that define the joy with which we began this chapter? Truly *it's the emotion evoked by well-being, success, or good fortune or by the prospect of possessing what we desire.* When we obey His law of love, we abide in Him, and as we continue in His Presence, He grants our requests. This revelation transformed my prayer life!

But there are other major benefits as well. In His Presence we more fully experience His joy which all by itself is simply marvelous. But wait, there's more: when we sow seeds of love we reap love, and nothing brings us more joy than sharing and receiving love. This is what truly fills our cup to overflowing (John 15:9-11). Science proves it. When we receive or offer love and a smile to another, our serotonin level increases. When a beloved dog sees it's master, it's serotonin level rises too. No wonder pets are easier to love than people. They can't hide their delight in us.

Want to Manifest Fullness of Joy?

Here's how this all works. Many people are dismayed because they don't feel God answers their prayers. In fact, the Bible teaches many principles on answered prayer. It says we must pray with faith (Mark 11:22-24) and according to His will (I John 5:14-15); that we can ask in His name (John 14:13-14), and that we must pray repeatedly until we get answers (cf. Luke 18:1-8). Finally, to get results, we must pray fervently and effectually (James 5:16). But perhaps the greatest key to praying effectually so we get the desired results is simply being in His Presence when we ask. Imagine asking someone for something in a crowded room when you are facing the wrong way and they are on the other side of the room. You probably won't get any response, let alone have your request granted. Yet many people approach prayer that way and get mad at God when they think He doesn't answer them.

If we want God to answer our prayers, we must first be in touch with Him. If we don't make contact it's like dialing up someone on a cell phone and never pushing the send button or hanging up before they answer. Sure He is omnipresent (everywhere). Surely He will never leave us, but that doesn't mean that just because you're talking He's listening. Scripturally, you can only be positive that He hears you when you abide in His Presence (John 15). That's what Jesus told us. True disciples can get whatever they request if they obey His commands to love and abide in Him (John 15:7-10). Your joy is full because you both enjoy Him and you enjoy His answers to all your requests.

I first learned some things about this from Gregg Braden. He teaches people to understand their spiritual journey in light of modern insights from quantum physics. He tells the story of a Native American friend who invited him along as he went to intercede for rain. Their region had been in a severe draught that appeared as if it would never end.

They went into a special prayer room to "pray rain." When his friend told him that, Gregg said, "Don't you mean pray for rain?" The man replied, "No, if we pray for rain we won't get it." Then he showed him how to 'pray rain'. For a long time he simply silently envisioned himself standing on a nearby street corner in a downpour. He imagined this until he could smell, feel and even taste what it felt like to be drenched in heavy rain. Once he was convinced that he truly believed without any doubt that it would rain (Mark 11:22-24), they left. Later that day it began to pour. It didn't stop until the draught was broken.

As an aside, I got the same results recently when I did the same thing during the worst draught in recorded history in Southern California. It soon stormed so hard we had our first hurricane forecast in recorded history. I entered His presence and prayed fervently against that and it swiped past us with little or no damage or human harm.

Years earlier, the day after I learned about 'praying rain', I faced a financial shortfall in my ministry. I decided to 'pray money'. As I lay on my bed and quieted my heart, I began to envision what it would feel like to have our need for money met. While in the Lord's Presence, a wealthy friend came to mind. I thanked the Lord that He seemed to be saying He would provide, and perhaps use my friend. When I got up, I tried to call my friend but there was no answer. I intended to ask for a $6,000 donation. The friend didn't know I tried to call because I didn't leave a message and my phone number is private so it was blocked on the receiver. Later that day I received an email telling me that a check for $10,000 -- 40% more that I prayed -- was in the mail to my ministry from that very same friend. It was my first experience of praying a truly believing prayer from deep within His Presence. When we pray while abiding in His Presence, our specific request or something better has been granted and our joy made full (John 15:11).

How to Put the Joy Back into Rejoicing

Finally, any discussion of joy would be incomplete if I did not also discuss rejoicing. We are called to rejoice in many things. This is good news because it again underscores the fact that our joy doesn't depend on circumstances. We can be proactive; ***we can choose to rejoice.*** We can respond to life positively rather than react to it negatively. We can even rejoice in temptations and trials (James 1:2), knowing that they perfect us so that we truly lack absolutely nothing (verse 4). This is not our natural reaction to trials; it's a mature, informed spiritual response. Trials and temptations are ultimately worthwhile because they leave us more whole and complete.

The word holiness - which really means being perfected in love just as God loves – does not come from some instantaneous sanctifying experience, as great as such experiences are. During the charismatic renewal in the Jesus Movement, many people called this the Full Gospel: being baptized in the Holy Spirit as a second work of grace beyond being reborn. For many, I think they needed this because they hadn't been born again when they were baptized in water or said the sinners' prayer. I believe that ***just like healing, perfection in love is a heroic lifetime journey.*** John Wesley was the only theologian I'm aware of who taught that we could be ***perfect in love in this life***. On his death bed, friends crowded around. One asked if he made it to perfection. He simply smiled and died.

The great good news is that even our struggles, problems and -- dare I say it -- stubborn besetting sins can move us closer to our eternal destination. We're encouraged to rejoice when we encounter trials and temptations because "the testing of your faith produces patience. But let patience have its perfect work, that you should be perfect (mature) and complete, lacking nothing" (James 1:2-4). Though you will seldom hear sermons on this, even Solomon, a veritable fount of godly wisdom, warned us not to be overly righteous lest we destroy ourselves, (Ecclesiastes 7:16). ***He well understood the perils of perfectionism.*** It's a killer that fosters a cold sterile rigid religiosity that inhibits all that God does to make us truly loving and righteous.

Lots of people like to say they are spiritual but not religious. I say I'm *Christian* but not religious. We all want to distant ourselves as much as possible from the censorious and hyper critical self-righteousness of superficial prudes. I love Martin Luther's stunning comment when he said ***"Sin boldly but believe and rejoice in Christ more boldly still."***

Henry Drummond, the aforementioned scientist, colleague and friend of DL Moody, said, ***"Above all, do not resent temptation: do not be perplexed because it seems to thicken round you more and more, and ceases neither for effort nor for agony nor prayer. That is the practice which God appoints you; and it is having its work in making you patient, and humble, and generous, and unselfish, and kind, and courteous".*** He continues, ***"Do not grudge the hand that is molding the still too shapeless image within you. It is growing more beautiful though you see it not, and every touch of temptation may add to its perfection. Therefore, keep yourself in the midst of life."*** He went on to say that ***"Character develops in the stream of the world's life. That chiefly is where men learn to love."*** See why Drummond's book, *THE*

GREATEST THING IN THE WORLD, is one of my favorite Christian books of all time?

I was judgmental and lacking compassion until I had to face my stubborn 'besetting' sins. As I struggled with my own lust, anger, impatience and unloving attitudes, I softened like meat being gently tenderized by the ethereal spiritual powder of God's grace. I gradually became more tolerant and merciful towards the shortcomings of others, and that's exactly how I should be.

Many years ago, a major evangelist felt called to visit with another world known evangelist and confront him over his inability to stop smoking cigars. As he told the man this, the smoker got up, walked around his desk and without saying a word, silently plunged his finger into the first man's obese belly. As the story goes, the first man stood up, indicated he got the message and the topic never again came up between them.

We all have our 'besetting sins', as the Apostle Paul called them. Sometimes when I speak to Christian groups I'll ask if there is anyone in the room who does not have something in their life they don't want anyone to know about. So far, not one person has ever raised a hand.

I cringe when I hear preachers say God can't bless you if there's sin in your life. That unbiblical teaching has squelched the efforts of countless people to dare to be great for God. Sure, there is a scripture that says if I regard iniquity in my heart He won't hear me (Psalm 66:18), but iniquity is different from sin. ***Sin is aiming at a far off target and falling short of it.*** Unconfessed sins can keep us from enjoying, experiencing and reflecting God's glory and radiating His love. That's why people should silently confess any unconfessed sins before they receive communion. I call it God's oil change for the soul. ***Iniquity is far worse.*** *It's deliberate intentional unrepentant evil. The dictionary defines iniquity as 'gross injustice or wickedness, a violation of a right or duty or a wicked act.' It's a lot more serious than some stubborn sin that you haven't yet overcome. If God can't bless sinners, He can't bless anyone!* Noah got drunk, Jacob and Abraham lied, Moses committed murder, Rahab was a prostitute, David had an affair and killed the woman's husband to cover it up, yet years later the Bible said David was a man after God's heart. Need I go on? I believe the Bible is the only religious text that reveals the stories of its greatest leaders, warts and all. If God used those sinners, He can surely use you and me. Jesus' very life proves that He is the Friend of sinners. Sadly, first century Pharisees demeaned and hated Him for it. They still do today. It's high time we realize that God didn't appoint us to judge "another man's servant" (Romans 14:4-10).

My favorite magazine in seminary was *The Wittenberg Door* - an irreverent Christian *Mad Magazine* that poked fun at the silly sanctimonious excesses in American church life. In one issue they took on what they called the *Theological Cosa Nostra* – self-righteous ministries that tear down anyone whose doctrine doesn't measure up to their rigid narrow standard. Such 'ministries' can cause grave damage to others. Recently one of these ministries interviewed a Chinese Christian who spent over 20 years in jail because the pseudo religious critique of their ministry by an American radio preacher gave the Communists an excuse to label him a dangerous cult. Endless attacks on other ministries won't hasten the establishment of God's Kingdom, it just temporarily helps religious cult leaders. In fact such sermons work inhibit God's coming Kingdom. ***The world will know Christ was sent of God by our unity (John 17:20-23).*** Is it any wonder so many people today doubt His divinity? Honestly, I also judged pastors harshly until God called me to try and do better!

We're commanded not to speak evil of anyone (Titus 3:2). The toxic perfectionistic messages of some pastors and ministries must stop. It only compounds people's struggles with sin. ***The strength of sin is the law*** (I Corinthians 15:56). Instead of being laced with true grace, messages laden with guilt throw people under the bus called "the law of sin and death" (Romans 8:2), accelerating their descent into depravity. ***Sin cannot dominate our life if we live under grace (Romans 6:14).***

I had a counseling client who struggled for over 30 years with self-hatred because he occasionally viewed pornography and he couldn't overcome the temptation. His life had become empty, his ministry fruitless, his family miserable all because of the spiritual cloud he was under. Twelve Step groups didn't work, (they fail 74% of the time), counseling and accountability to others failed him, and all his efforts to repent were painfully temporary. Until he could receive God's grace as freely as it's given (I John 1:9) he could never overcome. I taught him to be transformed by renewing his mind (Romans 12:1-2) through meditating on scriptures related to mercy, grace and forgiveness. He finally saw the light at the end of that 30 year tunnel and it wasn't an oncoming train! In a few weeks he had finally new peace and real victory in his life. *Please remember this:*

God isn't a perfectionist, He's a perfect Father. He doesn't need me to be good so He can look good, He IS good.

God looks on my heart, not my outer behavior. When I give myself to purifying my heart, my life and behavior improve almost effortlessly. After all, the evil that defiles us comes from our heart. As our inner life is washed in the water of God's Word, our whole life improves. The blood of Jesus Christ coursing through our spiritual veins can cleanse us from all sin. ***And the only thing we must do to keep that blood pure is confess (I John 1:5-9).*** A pastor I knew was on his knees begging forgiveness for something he'd done and confessed yours earlier. As he stopped beating himself up and started once again to say, "Lord, remember when I-" the Lord interrupted him and said, "No! I don't remember, because when I forgive I forget."

Some people fear that if they accept God's grace as freely as it's given, they will get worse. The opposite is true. When we let our heavenly Father love us warts and all, the grime dries up and falls off on its own. God's grace is truly sufficient; it works like Compound W on our spiritual warts).

Eugene Peterson says, "As a young pastor, I had little

patience with pietism – fussy devotional practices that separated its practitioners into conclaves of self-righteousness. I was bored with moralism – bromidic Reader's Digest versions of false spirituality that counsels us on how to live safe and sound." This echoes the sentiments of the Apostle Paul who warned us against behavior modification that appears godly but is "of no value against the indulgence of the flesh" (Colossians 2:23).

If the Bible teaches us anything it's that authentic Christianity is seldom boring and certainly not safe. Godly people lived life boldly, with a ferocious fearlessness, and I don't just mean Daniel when he survived the lion's den or David slaying Goliath. The Apostle Paul was stoned and left for dead on more than one occasion. Legend has Peter crucified upside down at his own request. He felt himself unworthy of being crucified right side up like Jesus was. All but one of the original apostles were martyred. Joshua used a divinely unconventional approach to conquering over 30 nations of fierce giants and warriors in order to subjugate and conquer the Promised Land. *Foxes Book of Martyrs* is packed with stories throughout history where Christians demonstrated the kind of courage that can only manifest in people who know that they possess eternal life and a better future rewards them.

These people didn't just hand out bulletins on Sunday morning and stir up trouble in church board meetings, no sir. God's greatest saints lived life vigorously and their moral lapses were legendary. Just consider how God used David with Bathsheba to bring us Solomon - who came from that union. Consider Solomon's hundreds of concubines and ungodly wives, which taught him much of the benevolent wisdom he left us. Or Rahab the harlot who helped God's people and is mentioned in the "faith hall of fame" in Hebrews 11. Obviously God has bigger fish to fry than our bad habits. He has a Kingdom to establish; one that will make earth heavenly; one that will increase without end until time stops and a new heaven and earth supplant the old. All of which which reminds me of another favorite bumper sticker from the Jesus movement: ***"Got guts? Follow Jesus."***

Christianity is not a namby-pamby religion reserved for the timid and tame. Biblical meekness has nothing to do with milquetoast; it's the gentle touch of a strong hand. And the strength we need comes from uninhibited joy, not from fearfully shrinking back from life and praying to escape before the shooing starts. When Marin Luther counseled us to sin boldly, he knew that God's grace was sufficient for his sin as well as the Apostle Paul's. He truly was the chief of all sinners for he tried to abort the early church. He also knew that just like us he would need that grace again and again.

So will you. And it's there for you, and not just before you become a Christian but every day thereafter. His joy is a very real part of all that: one that empowers us to risk living out His highest purpose for us. In the midst of a terrible trial don't forget to smile. It will make your enemies (and if you follow Jesus you will have some) very nervous.

Want Even More Bliss?

This chapter would be incomplete if I didn't mention Jesus' most important teaching on Joy: the Beatitudes. But what does that word even mean? Beatitude comes from the Latin *beatus* meaning blessed. These incomprehensible sayings from the Sermon on the Mount (Cf. Matthew 5:1-12) are often called ***BE Attitudes***. To be or not to be is not the question; *How* to be: that is the question. The Beatitudes describe the character traits we must develop if we are to experience the delectable yet elusive lifestyle we call bliss. If you want to be blessed so much you become blissful, the Beatitudes tell us exactly how you must live.

I studied the Bible for a long time before I began to probe the enigmatic meaning of the Beatitudes. Crazy, huh? I trust Jesus, I believe He spoke pure truth and I desperately want a blessed life, so what took me so long? I don't know, but I'm certain of this: when I decided to meditate on theses passages daily so I could comprehend how to incorporate them into my character, my life immediately began to become more blissful.

Many have written about the beatitudes but this is how I approached them and more importantly what I learned. Since there are only eight of them, I figured it wouldn't be hard to commit them to memory, but I hate memorizing so I took this simple shortcut: I reduced each one into a single word and meditated on each one daily every morning and night until they began reveal the things I needed to change and become more blissful.

The first thing I noticed is that each beatitude is counter-intuitive; they all seem to be the opposite of what we would consider blessed. It's just one more way in which everything in God's Kingdom is upside down.

Four of the beatitudes start with the letter P, three start with M and one starts with R. PPPP MMMR: This made it easy to remember them. The P words say blessed are the Poor, Pure, Peacemaker and Persecuted. See why I say they're counter-intuitive? Have you ever hoped to be persecuted? Have you yearned for Purity, embraced Poverty or ever longed to become a Peacemaker? It's common knowledge that cops who break up domestic disturbances are the ones who get physically attacked most often. Peacemaking forces in civil wars are usually attacked by both sides.

Moving right along, our whole society says we should aspire to be rich. How is poverty blissful? Society also seems to commend overt sensuality, the very opposite of purity as the best means to attain bliss. Do the beatitudes make natural carnal sense? Hardly.

So what about the M words? Blessed are the Meek, the Merciful and those who Mourn. Seriously? Who wants to be a milquetoast? What's so great about Mourning the loss of a loved one or object we cherish? And Merciful? We spend far more time justifying our position and rationalizing why it's someone else's fault then we ever do taking blame and accepting responsibility, don't we?

Maybe the R word is better. Blessed are those who are famished and dying of thirst because they aren't Righteous enough. Is that what it's saying? Doesn't our whole culture loathe self-righteousness? How can we ever make rational sense out of these eight 'blissful' behavioral qualities?

As I reflected daily on each of these simple words, they began to come into focus for me in a few weeks. Fortunately I knew enough Greek and Hebrew that some words created hidden epiphanies more easily than others. Some forced me to delve more deeply into the original meanings using commentaries. (These days those tools are readily available online so any can access them on their computer or smart phone, even if you don't know any Hebrew or Greek.)

Please allow me to start with the M words and distill the essence of what I discovered. Mourning actually made some sense. My grandfather died when I was ten years old and he was the most important person in my life. Throughout my teens and early twenties, I kept wishing he were still alive to guide me and show me the way. He was never far from my thoughts even after I became an adult. It took me 22 years to stop mourning for him. That happened at a Christian men's retreat when a big bear of a man gave me a hug and held on. The dam inside my heart finally broke and I cried my eyes out as the Holy Spirit touched the deepest part of my being. You see, Grandpa died in his sleep one night and had never even been sick. One day he was there, the next he was gone. I never got to grieve his passing. The man at the retreat resembled my grandfather and was taller than me so his hug finally released me to mourn. Afterwards I felt a massive relief. I still miss him and always will, but I finally experienced the blessing of mourning my grandpa. We all experience many losses in life: friendships, mates, jobs, pets, status, material stuff, all kinds of things. And society has taught us not to cry. We need to let ourselves mourn them all. God gave us tears but people take them away. "Big boys don't cry', we're taught. Or 'If you don't stop crying I'll give you something to cry about.'

Our WASP-ish society is packed with paltry platitudes. Tears actually release toxic chemicals from our mind, body and soul. Only then can the dark clouds of hurt be dispelled and the sunshine enter again in the depths of our soul. Only then can our grief be good. At our Transformational Healing seminar, when we give people permission to cry, they leave looking and feeling five years younger, and some instantly experience healing from physical diseases. Medical doctors acknowledge that as many as 95% of diseases are rooted in unhealed emotional pain. The psychiatric medical director of a treatment clinic where I conducted my seminar told me, "We knew unhealed emotional pain was the root cause of addictions. You showed us how to heal it." (My book *PEACE WITHOUT PROZAC* is a self healing workbook that I wrote to help you do that. *TRANSFORMATIONAL HEALING* specifically applies God's end time healing from Jeremiah 30 to heal the roots of addiction.)

Mercy was easier to comprehend. I've always known that *Hessed*, the Hebrew word for Mercy, is much bigger than just forgiveness. As I mentioned earlier, the only English word that does it justice is Lovingkindness. The mercy of the Lord endures forever. That phrase echoes throughout the entire Bible. Psalm 136 ends all 26 verses with that phrase! When God looks at us, no matter what we've done, He views us through the lens of lovingkindness. Isn't that a beautiful thought? If I want more lovingkindness in my life I must be more like God: I must indiscriminately share His spiritual affection with others. When I try to pass that on to people throughout my day, it works wonders. Earth truly visits heaven in even my most casual of relationships. It's so rare in life that as people are treated that way when I pass it on, they usually soak it up and can't help but give some back. Yes, ere again our serotonin level increases when we do this and it makes us feel better too.

What about Meekness, how does that work? In our technological age I can almost see how the geeks inherit the earth, but what causes the meek to receive this too? The Bible defines meekness as "An attitude of humble, submissive and expectant trust in God, and a loving, patient and gentle attitude towards others." I gotta tell ya', that just doesn't come naturally for me! As an only child, I like getting my own way, and when someone cuts me off on the freeway or won't let me have my way I can almost feel the hair bristling on the back of my neck. But when I indulge that reaction I never get what I want. When I was in college I got three traffic tickets in a few months. No matter what I did I couldn't talk my way out of any of them. When I got pulled over the fourth time I knew better; I was far more humble. Amazingly, I got off with a warning! Even when we "resist not evil' it usually moves consequences in the direction we prefer! I've been far more humble in my daily encounters with people since I began meditating on meekness and you know what? Even if I don't get exactly what I want it still feels a whole lot better than all the prideful bluster I can muster.

I didn't have much trouble understanding Righteousness and how that fills us up; after all, I wrote a whole chapter on it. But those P words are quite another story. Just before I became a Christian I had been the highest paid executive trainee of a Fortune 500 company and I was miserable. By the time I gave my life to the Lord I was just about broke and if I'd had any other options I probably wouldn't have caved in to Him, but once I did, I was exuberantly happy just basking in God's unconditional love. That one kinda made sense. For me, that was the treasure buried in the field of God's Kingdom; the buried treasure for which I'd given everything to possess. But how could I be blessed by being persecuted? Talk about counterintuitive, we spend much of our life trying to make people think well of us, and this is saying we should rejoice when people want to harm us? We can all get defensive when someone misrepresents what we said. Now we're supposed to rejoice when they falsely accuse us?

As I reflected on this mystery I realized that some people I dearly loved had accused me of doing evil things I never would have done. And though I could prove that to them they still wouldn't let me off the hook. I nursed those unjust wounds almost every day and never felt any better. But once I realized I was in great company, that prophets and apostles and great saints throughout history had similarly suffered for their dedication to God and living truthfully, I didn't feel so bad. Even Jesus said a prophet is not without honor except in his own home and town. At one point, even His relatives thought Him crazy. That's when He said His true family are those who do God's will. And as soon as I released my hurt and decided to love these dear folks anyhow, their attitude towards me softened and they began to change. Isn't it great how scriptural truth works!

Now Purity and Peacemaking, those were another story. Then I realized the Bible is talking about Purity of heart. Theologian Soren Kierkegaard wrote a book entitled *Purity of Heart is to Will One Thing*. In it he spoke of the purity of purpose that comes from placing God's will above all else. Once I embraced that my whole motivation changed. I stopped going to parties to have fun and meet new people and instead went there to do my best to let the Lord love people through me. And WOW- Wonder Of Wonders: I began to see Him in every person with whom I engaged in conversation. And you know what? That was a lot more fun. Funny thing is, now when I go to parties I often end up with a small group of people clustered around me talking about stuff that really matters and we all have a ball.

I got the Peacemaking thing. It wasn't talking about cops getting between feuding spouses or troops stopping genocide. This one came pretty easy for me. As I shared earlier, scriptural Peace is that glorious word Shalom, a greeting pregnant with the greatest blessings we could ever desire. For over 45 years I've led Spiritual Growth Retreats, and over the last 30 years I've conducted

Transformational Healing Retreats and Seminars. The motto for these events is ***Change Your Life in a Weekend***. That really happens for people, and it is pure joy to be an instrument of God's Peace in that way. Recently I attended a gathering of people I hadn't seen in seven or eight years. I was surprised by how much older and heavier they looked. As I was leaving a man stopped me and said, "How is it we haven't seen you in years and you showed up looking younger and better than ever?" I laughed and told him, "People don't believe me when I tell them they will look five years younger after one of my retreats. I guess I owe it to that."

I've not done those events for years but I'm starting to do them again, and few things in all of life are more rewarding. Even better, my Best Friend said if I tell people He's renewing my youth like an eagle, ***He will keep renewing my youth***. As I write this I feel better than I did 35 years ago and most people tell me I look 20 or 30 years younger. I'd be a billionaire if I could bottle that!

So all eight Beatitudes can lead us to bliss if we let them. Want to be more blessed? Jesus told us what we need to do, and even though it doesn't make sense in the natural, I'd much rather embrace the spiritual. It truly works.

> *"If you keep my commandments you will abide in My love, just as I have kept My Father's commandments and abide in His love. These things I have spoken to you, that My joy may remain in you, and that your joy may be full'"*
> *– John 15:10-11*

"I will turn their mourning into joy." – Jeremiah 31:13

"In Your presence is fullness of joy; at Your right hand are pleasures forevermore." – Psalm 16:11

DISCUSSION QUESTIONS

Describe joy in your own words.

____

____

____

____

____

What would bring more joy into your life?

____

____

____

____

____

What sacrifices would that require of you? Is it worth it?

____

____

____

____

____

CHAPTER TEN

KEY SIX: THE ULTIMATE SACRIFICE - WELL WORTH IT?

"If anyone comes to Me and does not hate his father and mother, wife and children, brothers and sisters yes, and his own life also, he cannot be my disciple." – Luke 14:26

"He who does not take his cross and follow Me is not worthy of Me. He who finds his life will lose it, and he who loses his life for My sake will find it." – Matthew 10:38-39

THOUGH I'VE OFTEN SAID THAT most of us have heard too many sermons on sacrifice, God's Kingdom cannot be ours without it. However, it helps if we understand why it's necessary and how and why we're supposed to make those supreme sacrifices. Like every Kingdom mandate, these requirements aren't arbitrary; they are true Truth, based on the very nature of reality. They enable and empower us to obtain the abundant life which Jesus came to give us.

By now it should be obvious why Jesus likened His Kingdom to buried treasure that's so precious you would gladly sell everything to obtain it (Matthew 13:45-6). In truth, we must sacrifice all that we have and all that we are in order to gain the full benefits of His Kingdom. When we connect with God, we learn in a whole new way the pronouncement of Francis of Assisi who said "It is in giving that we receive."

This is yet another example of why everything in God's Kingdom is upside down. You're called to love your enemies, not hate them. All religions teach that you should love your neighbor, but this commandment separates Christianity from every other religion. Only scriptural Christianity has the audacity to challenge us to love our enemies. That's because it's the only 'religion' that gives us the personal power to love our enemies. We can do this because Jesus did. Jesus could because He had the power to conquer death. And death to self is small compared to that. The same power that raised Him from the dead resides in us; the very same Holy Spirit that birthed Him can rebirth us. The same Spirit that enabled Jesus to forgive His torturers for "they know not what this do" can surely help us find compassion for those who do far less to us.

So how does this work? If someone takes your coat you're supposed to give them your cloak as well. If they hit you, you're commanded to turn the other cheek. These aren't natural reactions they are spiritual responses, and they really work. It's God's way of fighting fire with water. Soft answers turn away wrath, gentleness defuses violence, and gifts to thieves have been known to turn around their lives. At the very least they keep victims from being murdered over mere property.

The ultimate example of this upside-down kingdom is the one piece of baggage that Jesus encouraged us to carry. When we embark on *His* path, we must also take up our own personal cross in order to follow Him. As the martyr Dietrich Bonhoeffer so rightly proclaimed, "When Christ calls us to follow Him He bids us come and die!"

Our cross isn't just a tiresome burden we must bear like an affliction, birth defect or lack in our upbringing, social status or looks. It defines how we should live our daily lives (I Corinthians 15:31). Jesus knew that unless a seed goes into the ground and dies it abides alone, but if it dies, it bears much fruit (John 12:24). And as we've seen, He wants us all to live fruitful meaningful lives. We can't truly be His disciples unless we do (John 15:8).

When the rich young ruler asked Jesus' advice on how to be godly He didn't tell him to tithe. He said that if he wanted to be perfect, he should sell everything and give to the poor. Does this mean Jesus expects us all to be paupers as the Jainism religion teaches? Hardly. If God intended that for everyone, the Bible wouldn't have taught us how to prosper and become rich (cf. Proverbs chapter 8 and dozens of other verses. A simple web search reveals over 70 scripture passages explaining what we must do to prosper. Jesus well understood that wealth can become the root of all kinds of evil (I Timothy 6:10); that it could blind us from seeing what was truly important and having a holistically rich life worthy of His kingdom. Money could actually rob us of the abundant life He wants for each of us (John 10:10). But Jesus knew that the rich young ruler was possessed by his possessions. And while we may not all be called to literally sell everything, He still clearly taught that unless we **forsake all we have we cannot be His disciples**. Note, He didn't say He wouldn't allow us to be disciples. He said we simply aren't able to. At some time in our lives we will all be challenged to discern what this means for us.

On a few occasions I've had to forsake my all to follow His call. The first time I gave up that lucrative job as the highest paid executive trainee of a Fortune 500 company to clean bed pans in the geriatric ward of a psychiatric hospital for $1.60 an hour. This led to a job at a children's psychiatric hospital. There I was used for the first time in my life to heal someone, a teenage patient. I was so financially downwardly mobile I next worked my way into a position as the editor of an underground Christian newspaper for $10 a week while living in an inner city commune. That was my first foray into full time ministry and I've been doing that ever since in one way or another. I've also derived a satisfaction from following Him that no other vocation would ever provide. The Apostle Paul did too. Though he supported himself as a tent maker he said he was addicted to ministry.

Years later, the Lord called me to give up all earthly security and resign from my job as a pastor of a growing mainline church. I wasn't sure why, but I believed somehow He wanted to promote me. I had no job, no bank account, no house, no salary and very little savings or credit. I also had three small children and another due any day. Supernaturally, I ended up buying my dream house with instant equity of $45,000; the exact amount I lost by living in a parsonage for eight years. But had I not been willing to forsake all vestiges of earthly security, that couldn't have happened. I had to first step out in faith.

Yet another time, I was called to again forsake all security and move across country to pursue my dream of making quality crossover feature films that glorify God. Once again I had no job or income. Though I have yet to realize the payout on this venture I still know it's going to be great in more ways than one. Someone said 'God always gives his best to those who leave the choice to Him' and I believe that with all my heart. He's proven it to me time and time again.

Having said all that, I still think many Christians have heard far too many sermons on self-sacrifice. For a while, I wondered if all God wanted was to make us all impoverished dynamic doormats. I chafed at that and I fear that many people feel that way now. But over the years I learned that if we are called to die to ourselves or forsake our possessions and even our loved ones in a certain situation it's ultimately for our own good and there's as well as the good of God's Kingdom. Even Jesus endured the cross to receive the joy that came through the resurrection (Hebrews 12:2). I too have always found deep lasting joy on the far side of any self-mortification He has ever asked of me.

It's been said that when people marveled at the great sacrifices the famous missionary David Livingstone made to pursue his calling to Africa, he smiled, shook his head and said he had gotten far more than he had given up. I thought of that when I saw a TV show about a woman who had a doctorate in theology and gave up her plush life in Laguna Beach, one of the most elegant places on the west coast. She did it to move to Africa and train children to do healing ministry. Ten year old kids saw healing flow through their own hands on a daily basis. When asked about the sacrifice, her husband said, "What did we give up?" Standing in his tiny closet office, hemmed in by so many books he could barely turn around he said, "Look at all we have here. We see regular miracles at the hands of children. California had nothing to offer us as good as this."

Yet a purely religious mindset about self-sacrifice can be damaging. Years ago the great Bible teacher Bob Mumford said he'd rather be with a person who was *"wrong with the right spirit than one who was right with the wrong spirit."* I so get that. Those who were right with the wrong spirit were the ones who demanded Jesus' crucifixion. Those who were wrong with the right spirit were numbered amongst those grimy sinners He came to save. It's not for nothing that Jesus seemed more comfortable with lushes and loose women than with the puritanical perfectionistic Scribes and Pharisees.

This is a short chapter but an essential one if we're to apprehend the bliss of God's Kingdom. To be sure, Kingdom Christianity requires more of its followers than any major religion, but it also promises us a whole lot more, both in this life and the next. Those who think otherwise have missed something far better than eternal retirement benefits and ironically they may even miss those as well. It's not only well worth the huge apparent price tag, it's a bargain.

What about the opening passage for this chapter? Are we really called to hate our loved ones? Not all of them and not always. But Satan is a wily one. No one has more power to control us than our parents, mate, children, siblings and friends. If they try to compel us to stop following Jesus, we may need to develop a holy hatred in order to resist. My blind mother was so distraught over my early Christian commitment she grabbed a knife and swung it at me. It was easy to disarm her, but I finally knew that no explanation would convince her why I had to do crazy things like give up a great job and work for $10 a week in an inner city Christian commune. So I stopped trying to witness to her. Others can do that far better than loved ones. A short while later, my father came to see where I lived. By then I had moved to another joint living situation in an old inner city church during the Jesus movement. We held contemporary Christian music concerts to reach out to young people all over the city. When I went out to greet my dad he was weeping. ***It was the very same church where decades earlier he became a Christian as a teenager.*** He privately rededicated his life to Jesus. Months later he brought my mom to an evangelistic crusade in Cleveland stadium. After the message, I was counseling people who wanted to follow Jesus. Though I couldn't see my mom in the crowd, I knew she was there I also instinctively knew she gave her life to Jesus for the very first time that night.

> *"And everyone who has left houses or brothers or sisters or father or mother or wife or children or lands, for My name's sake, shall receive a hundredfold, and inherit everlasting life." – Matthew 19:29*
>
> *"I die daily." – The Apostle Paul, I Corinthians 15:31b*

DISCUSSION QUESTIONS

What sacrifices would you have to make if you took this chapter seriously?

____

____

Would it be worth it?

____

____

How would your life change for the better?

____

____

Does God want you prosperous or poor? What scriptures support this?

____

____

____

CHAPTER ELEVEN

KEY NUMBER SEVEN: HIS KINGDOM POWER WORKS THROUGH YOU

"But you will receive power when the Holy Spirit has come upon you, and you will be my witnesses in all Judea and Samaria, and to the end of the earth" (Acts 1:8).

Jesus told the Pharisees "You are wrong, because your know neither the scriptures nor the power of God" (Matthew 22:29).

JESUS DIDN'T JUST PREACH A GOOD STORY, He walked the talk. He demonstrated such dynamic spiritual power that His life transcended the impact of any other religious or secular figure in world history. What other miracle worker walked on water, turned it into wine or stopped powerful storms with his words? What other spiritual being healed all manner of diseases and cast out demons on demand? Who else restored the dead to life, conquered his own grave and proved it to those who saw Him die?

You can't read the gospels without seeing the

manifestation of Jesus' supernatural power. Forty percent of His ministry involved healing incurable diseases and delivering people from the horrifying grip of tormenting evil spirits. Wherever He went the lame walked, the blind saw, the deaf heard and demons panicked. He challenged His followers to do the same. ***So why don't we see more of this in the Church?***

Some atheists enjoy mocking our apparent impotence. They love to crow, 'If God heals why are hospitals so full? If He's the omnipotent God of peace, why are there so many wars?' It isn't God's fault. Jesus' earthly ministry was powerful beyond words and He expected His followers' ministry to be like that as well. Healing and deliverance (exorcism) were normal activities for the Apostles; just read the Book of Acts. They also raised the dead, just like Jesus said they would. And they impacted the planet like no other religion in history. In less than 400 years Christianity dominated the civilized world, and its expansion continues today in the third world where far more Christians manifest the supernatural. Over two billion people claim Christianity as their religion, about one fourth of the planet and more than any other religion. So what's wrong with western Christianity? Why isn't the Church growing here? A better question: American evangelicals adamantly defend the super- natural God of the Bible, so why don't we demonstrate His power today?

A large part of the blame must reside in our Bible schools and seminaries. Most merely teach clergy to study and talk. Hardly any have classes in physical, spiritual and emotional healing and deliverance. Some actively teach against healing and miracles, and I don't mean just liberal churches who decry the supernatural. Some fundamentalists deny the relevance and necessity of healing and deliverance. Hardly any train their students, elders and parishioners to exercise real spiritual power like Jesus did by casting out demons, healing the sick and liberating the wounded, yet this is the best evidence of God's kingdom coming in power and not just in words (I Corinthians 2:2-4). I was shocked to learn that even the Salvation Army, which regularly works with the lowest strata in society, doesn't teach their officers to heal or confront the demonic. And yet, the scriptures indicate this is a basic mandate of discipleship (Mark 16:15-18), and the whole world desperately needs it. God didn't do supernatural healing in the first century to launch the Church with a bang. He needs no PR. ***He did it because He is Love.*** It's no wonder that the churches that denounce God's power today are usually unloving, judgmental and shrinking.

If every church became a place where people could go to heal their brokenness, deal with their demons and pray for the sick with scriptural results, mental hospitals – perhaps all hospitals – would lose a lot of business. Great masses of people would be truly converted. The terrible cost of our health problems (19% of our national GNP) would be dramatically diminished, including over 100,000 people who die in hospitals each year because of doctor's mistakes. That's the third biggest killer in the USA, right behind heart disease and cancer. It's almost twice as many soldiers as were killed in the entire Viet Nam war. Our skyrocketing health costs and homeless problems could be substantially reduced if churches offered what Jesus did and commanded us to do. Yet the lack of such ministry is almost as omnipresent as God Himself. Ironically, it seems many churches want it that way.

Some years back, I was asked to consult with a large evangelical church because their men's group was spiritually dead. I met with their men and a core group of leaders for over a year. I then recommended a spiritual growth retreat to help their men gain love, support and nurture from close authentic relationships with other Christian men. That way they could "build one another up in love" – as the Apostle Paul taught (Ephesians 4:11-16).

In his enthusiasm for our plans, the leader of the group asked me to send an email to the 5,000 men on their church list, explaining who I was and our plans for the retreat. Though I questioned the wisdom of this strategy, I did as he requested. Some men who had no knowledge of all the things that led up to this planned retreat went to my website and discovered that I believed in healing. The outhouse hit the fan. They immediately pulled the plug on the event.

In a meeting with a church elder to understand what happened he asked me if it was true that I said we could do the things Jesus did. I said "No, I didn't say that, ***Jesus did***. In fact Jesus said that believers could not only do the things He did but also greater things" (John 14:12). He couldn't swallow that. The church pulled away from all efforts to truly help men grow spiritually and brought in a young fundamentalist evangelist for their men's retreat.

They then started a new 51 week Bible study on the book of Ephesians!

Sadly, this church tells people they believe in spiritual gifts. I think they said that because they wanted to keep Charismatics coming and donating. But they give no opportunities for the exercise of any real, powerful spiritual gifts. In fact, that churches' pastor believes in Dispensationalism, an unbiblical theological system. Though it defends the supernatural in the Bible (Moses parted the Red Sea, Jesus was born of a virgin, healed the sick and rose from the dead), it twists and distorts the scriptures to explain why the supernatural is no longer needed or relevant in today's 'dispensation'.

Dispensationalism denies the immutability of God - the clear biblical teaching that God never changes (Hebrews 13:8) - by using a method of biblical interpretation called Eisegesis. *Exegesis* seeks to get out of scripture what is in a given passage; *Eisegesis reads into scriptures something that isn't there.*

To explain why the supernatural is not operating in their ministries, they refer to the scripture that says that "tongues will cease" (meaning speaking in tongues), "when that which is perfect will come ... and that which is in part will be done away" (I Corinthians 13:8, 10). Though the Bible doesn't ever teach that miracles, healing and deliverance will be unnecessary, dispensationalists distort this verse to conclude that spiritual gifts stopped at some point in history. They say that the supernatural was only necessary to validate the ministry of Jesus and the Apostles and to establish the early Church. They argue that the perfect which was to come refers to the Bible, and that once we had that, there was no longer any need for God to speak to us through tongues, interpretations and prophecies or to perform miraculous healings or deliverance ministry. When they pray for the sick, they usually ask God to guide the doctor's hands.

Though the Bible explicitly says we should not forbid the use of spiritual gifts (I Corinthians 14:39), such churches do exactly that. Some go so far as to say that the spiritual gifts mentioned in the Bible (Romans 12:6-8, I Corinthians 12:1-11) are 'of the devil'. This allegation is frightfully close to that of the religious leaders who accused Jesus of casting out demons using Satan's power; a teaching He likened to the unforgivable sin of blasphemy against the Holy Spirit (Matthew 12:25-32).

Besides being unbiblical, the problem with this reasoning is that healing and deliverance were not done because they were necessary to establish the first century Church, they are expressions of God's love and power for a lost, afflicted and hurting humanity. They also reveal His power over His creation. After all, He who created the laws of nature can circumvent them whenever He pleases.

Not surprisingly, churches that embrace this doctrine usually care more about being right than loving, as if there will be a great spiritual SAT test in the sky to determine if we get into heaven. Jesus' standard is different. He separates the sheep from the goats (the righteous from the sinners) not on the basis of their intellectual assent to dogma, but because of the practical love they extend to the imprisoned, naked, hungry and homeless (Matthew 25:31-46).

Nationally known authors and TV and radio ministers still rail against healing and deliverance today, claiming it's not necessary or even possible any more. Some pastors refer their people to medical psychiatrists for destructive drugs and antidepressants that can lead to addiction, suicide and over 100 serious medical complications rather than learn about how Jesus is healing broken people today. Even some famous Christian psychiatrists recommend these same meds as a final solution. Today, certain seminaries and Bible colleges that say they believe in the Bible still teach against healing. They use unsound Bible interpretations to contravene the clear and simple mandates and examples of scriptures. Meanwhile millions of people take so many prescriptions even their doctors can't keep up with all the toxic interactions. Over $200 million is spent in America ***every day just on antidepressants***. H B London from Focus on the Family ministry estimates that half of American preacher's wives take prescription drugs. Sadly, those drugs became the fourth largest cause of death in America, also killing over 100,000 people per year.

These inconsistencies are hardly new. When Jesus announced that He was the One that Isaiah predicted would come to heal the broken and liberate the bruised, the members of his home synagogue were so irate they wanted to kill him (Luke 4:28-29). When He cast out demons, the religious leaders claimed he was doing the devil's work (Matthew 12:24). When He healed on the Sabbath they plotted to murder Him! (Cf. verse 14). With religious friends like these who needs enemies? No wonder Jesus hated false religion. Sadly, I believe religious demons are meaner than any based on sex, alcohol or illicit drugs.

The problem we face today is not that much different from the problem Jesus encountered in the first century. Decades ago, I was fired from my job at a children's' psychiatric hospital because a 13 year old patient on my ward got healthy enough to be released from the hospital. This was after he spent seven years in and out of the psychiatric ward for setting fires. How did he finally heal? He attended a hell fire and brimstone church as an infant. In kindergarten he got into trouble when he brought a plastic knife to school and threatened another student. From then on he was certain he was doomed to hell. I asked if that's why he set fires and he hung his head and nodded yes. He believed in the Bible, so I simply shared scriptures with him about God's love and forgiveness and prayed for him whenever he requested it. The psychiatrist was thrilled with the results and told me to keep it up. But a Presbyterian nurse said it was a violation of the separation of church and state. She initiated the process that led to my firing.

Flaky fundamentalism reared its ugly head again in a men's prison where I led a successful healing seminar. They forbade us to do the follow up healing with their inmates because during the seminar, I encouraged an inmate to imagine he was talking to his dead father as if he were alive so he could access the pain he had felt as a teen from that dysfunctional relationship. The chaplain accused me of using spiritualism.

Why is healing such a lightening rod? What motivates respected Christian leaders to speak against it? When psychiatric hospitals are jammed with people that drugs can't cure, why are emotional healing and demonic deliverance scorned and mocked?

In Christian circles, I believe many people are as threatened by their own impotence to heal as the Pharisees were in Jesus' day. The radio preacher who attacks healing doesn't do it on the basis of any responsible interpretation of scripture, but simply because he hasn't seen any healing in his ministry. My question to him would be this: if you tried to pray for the sick, did you use biblical methods? The book of James says if someone is sick, the elders should lead them in a time of mutual confession, and then pray effectual fervent prayer for healing (James 5:14-16). I wonder if he and his elders dare to be that humble, vulnerable and transparent. Are they capable of such *'effectual, powerful, fervent prayer'*? Did this famous radio pastor help his elders grow their faith strong enough so they could pray for healing without doubt that it will be done? Everything we ask for without doubt is done for us (Mark 11:22-24). If that isn't true, God is a liar.

Simple faith unlocks the key to healing. In Gregg Braden's book *The Divine Matrix,* he *tells of a hospital in communist China that has a 95% cure rate with supposedly incurable diseases.* They begin by changing people's nutrition and helping them access what they call *chi* energy, which may actually be the subconscious presence of the Holy Spirit. Then they have their trained practitioners minister to the patient. Whether they realize it or not, these "practitioners" are praying believing prayers over the patients.

Braden tells of seeing an amazing video of an ultrasound that shows a patient with an inoperable, incurable tumor. Four practitioners 'pray' over her, affirming words to the effect that "It is gone." "This is healed," and "It is accomplished." ***In a little over two and a half minutes, the tumor visibly shrinks and disappears as they do that!***

When I share that story, some Christians get offended because these people aren't "believers" and they didn't pray in Jesus' name. The fact is, they apparently have more faith than most Christian 'believers' do. And Jesus' name isn't a foolproof mantra; it's something available for Christians to use. Faith is the currency of God's Kingdom and when we pray in Jesus' name, it's like saying, "I'm buying this using God's credit card." But if we don't believe God will act, He seldom does. The simple fact is that Jesus said whatever we believe without doubt has already been done for us (Mark 11:22-24). And these communist Chinese practitioners do exactly that. I dare say they do so more than doctors in any western hospital where pseudo scientific skepticism reigns supreme. Sadly, they also get greater results than most pastors in American churches today. God always honors His Word so He responds to sincere faith, which these people are clearly exercising; and they are doing it effectually and fervently I might add.

So what about Demons?

Deliverance is similarly simple. A few years ago I spoke

on it in a church in Cleveland. When I was done, the pastor and his wife rushed up to me and said one thing I taught made everything clear to them. I just said that deliverance doesn't ever have to be a big, scary, hairy deal. The key to deliverance is to get the person who is demonically oppressed to renounce whatever gave the evil spirit access to him or her. The person must then determine that they want nothing to do with the lust, overeating, drugs, gossip, rage, fear, or other torment that has bound them up in a personal prison of compulsion, hopelessness and despair. Once he or she sincerely renounces it, the demon must leave at the believer's command. This is why I stress the need for counseling before and after any deliverance. That way you can get to the root of the problem and get it permanently resolved. Once that's done, the person can be totally free. However, until the person sincerely desires this freedom, deliverance is impossible and shouldn't be attempted. Sadly, many Christians believe Christians can't have a demon. Who would Satan try harder to infest?

Our world is so sick, even the church is bruised and wounded and our medical system is broken almost beyond repair. Today's world desperately longs for real, supernatural manifestations of tangible power in the Church. When they don't find it they often reject "organized religion." It's no wonder so many people call themselves spiritual but not religious.

When religion attacks those who try to do "the things Jesus did and greater"; when it condemns those who believe the Church should do more than just preach and teach; when it rails against people who believe every word Jesus spoke is true and relevant for today, it deserve to become irrelevant. Life is too short and serious to waste on those who call themselves believers while they undermine effectual faith in the supernatural God.

I wonder if those who say that healing, miracles and deliverance from evil spirits is unnecessary today have spent any time inside a modern psychiatric hospital, or even a few hours in an intensive care ward or a doctor's waiting room. Healing, miracles and deliverance are as needed today as ever before and nothing in the Bible says they won't be. In fact, the Lord's promise to heal the pain of His people is especially relevant in the last days (Jeremiah 30:12-24). My book, *Peace Without Prozac*, shows you exactly how to do that. It can equip you and your church for the end time healing the world so desperately needs and that God ordains in Jeremiah 30:24. As an aside, when I served on my counties' prescription drug coalition, the District Attorney spoke with us about the problem of Opioids. She also told us that instead of having the best medical system in the world, the US ranks 50th among developed nations. When I asked why, she said we are the only developed country that allows prescription companies to advertise on TV and radio. Consequently, if a doctor doesn't prescribe a drug the patients don't feel he did his job.

I understand people's desire to explain away the miraculous. What sincere pastor hasn't prayed for healing only to see people grow worse and perhaps even die? But again, the problem is not with God. Tremendous healings and miracles are being performed in Jesus' name even by children in other less 'well-informed' parts of the world. I've personally helped over 40 people heal from incurable diseases. It's only here in the 'educated' skeptical West that miracles are so sparse. Many of us have been 'brain-dirtied' to believe that the supernatural is impossible.

Those churches, schools and denominations that preach against such things cannot point to one scripture that proves that the supernatural is not for today. The scriptures clearly affirm that Jesus is the same yesterday, today and forever (Hebrews 13:8). This scripture became the foundation for the ministry of Aimee Semple McPherson, probably the greatest healer since Christ and the only woman to from a major denomination. Everywhere she went the blind saw, the deaf heard and the lame walked. The American Medical Association investigated and tried to discredit her but concluded that her ministry was valid and real; proven miracles regularly occurred.

They can happen again in America today. In some places they are. Christian 'Healing Rooms' are springing up all over the country to do the supernatural work the Church refuses to do. In the last century, John G. Lake had healing rooms in Spokane Washington. They prayed in person and remotely with any who requested it in letters or telegrams. Over 100,000 people a year received those prayers and Spokane became the healthiest city in America.

The Bible clearly teaches that God's Kingdom comes with power, not just words. Mere talk is way too cheap. His disciples today are still mandated to heal and cast out demons, even the ones who sometimes dominate church and denominational board meetings. Just imagine what would happen if we did that. We just might exorcise the evil powers that keep the church so impotent and irrelevant. His people just might be sufficiently healed to make disciples again and take the wonderful good news of His Kingdom to the ends of the earth, ***teaching all people to obey all things He commanded, including healing the sick and setting the captives free.*** If that happens, His Kingdom would surely have finally come to earth.

> *"And these signs will follow those who believe: in my name they will cast out demons, and they will speak with new tongues; and they will take up deadly serpents; and if they drink any deadly thing, it will by no means hurt them; they will lay hands on the sick and they will recover." – Mark 16:17-18*

> *"Most assuredly I say to you, he who believes in Me, the works that I do and greater works than these he will do, because I go to My Father." – John 14:12*

> *"Nevertheless, when the Son of Man comes, will He really find faith?" – Luke 18:8b*

A simple web search for every passage in the Bible on healing will give you all the keys you need to understand how to help people heal.

DISCUSSION QUESTIONS

Would you like to see Kingdom power demonstrated more in your life? If so, in what way?

____
____
____
____
____

What would you do with this power if you use it? Be practical.

____
____
____
____
____

What must you learn and do to accomplish this?

____
____
____
____
____

CHAPTER TWELVE

KINGDOM PARABLES

Jesus said, "The knowledge of the secrets of the kingdom of God has been given to you, but to others I speak in parables, so that, 'though seeing, they may not see; though hearing, they may not understand.'" – Luke 8:10.

HAVING EXPLORED THE SEVEN MAJOR KEYS of God's Kingdom, it's time to consider God's Kingdom message in Jesus' parables. Almost half of them explore the gospel of the Kingdom. Forget about a new world order, they explain how God's World Order is intended to work. First here's a brief primer for studying parables in general and the Kingdom parables in particular. It will help you glean more of the great good news that's revealed in the most salient points from each parable.

As mentioned, God's Kingdom appears 155 times in the New Testament. This includes 124 passages in the gospels and 31 more verses beyond the gospels. Matthew and Luke each refer to the Kingdom 44 times, the most of any books in the Bible. Mark referenced the Kingdom 20 times while John's gospel shares the least, only five times.

Believe it or not, some Christians claim the gospels are aimed at Jews and use that as an excuse to reject Jesus' commandments. But the Apostle Paul, who is known as the Apostle to Gentiles (non-Jews) explained the Kingdom gospel 14 times in his epistles! In addition, the book of Acts mentioned it eight times, and Revelations five times. Hebrews mentions it twice, and James and Peter each once. Matthew is the only writer to call it the Kingdom of Heaven. That's because he ministered primarily to Jews. They refrained from using God, so as not to risk 'taking the Lord's name in vain'. All other biblical authors who reached out to more Gentiles refer to it as the Kingdom of God.

God's Kingdom was Jesus' favorite topic in His parables.

Of the 42 unique parables in the New Testament, 19 explain the Kingdom. Matthew used 15 parables to explore God's blessed Kingdom, Mark used it four and Luke six. That's 25 times it's mentioned instead of 19 because some authors used the same parable in their gospel as other authors. But it serves to further validates the essential message of Jesus' Kingdom gospel.

None of John's three parables explore God's Kingdom. This might seem strange since John apparently knew Jesus more intimately than the other disciples, but his gospel is markedly different from the synoptic gospels, which provide us with a synopsis of Jesus' ministry and teachings. John, was known as the beloved disciple because he offers us a deeper understanding of Jesus' character, personality and life.

As we'll see, Matthew, Mark and Luke bear a striking similarity to each other. Most biblical scholars believe they borrowed from each other. Many conclude that though Mark's gospel is the shortest in length, it was probably the first gospel written. They theorize that both Matthew and Luke adapted Mark's pattern and enriched it with their respective memories and anecdotes.

Though he doesn't offer us any Kingdom parables, John's close friendship with Jesus yields amazing insights. He quotes perhaps the most important verse in the Bible on the Kingdom. In John 3:5 Jesus informs us that unless we are born again we can neither see nor enter God's Kingdom. Why? God's Kingdom truly is both an internal and eternal Kingdom (Luke 17:21). A major insight Luke gave us is two fold: the word Jesus used for God's Kingdom within means it's both intimately personal and relationally among us through other Christ followers. So unless our spiritual blindness is healed through the Holy Spirit and our inner eyes of the heart are opened we can't even perceive His Kingdom. If we can't see it, how can we possibly enter it? If it's among us in other Christ followers, we must honor them as spiritual siblings and joint heirs of God's Kingdom. Sometimes their perceptions may be better than ours and vice versa. All who seek to follow Jesus truly need the other parts of Christ's body as well as their gifts, ministries and callings.

Parenthetically, Jehovah's witnesses name their churches Kingdom Halls because they claim to stress the Kingdom message which the larger church ignores. But they don't believe we must be born again, hence they can't envision His Kingdom accurately. Consequently, their legalism keeps their own people from seeing and receiving the true Kingdom gospel.

Many years ago, I was speaking to a group of Christian leaders about being radically devoted to Jesus. I invited the wife of a high school friend who had recently become a Jehovah's Witness. I wore a cross necklace. Her hand shot up during Q and A. I called on her first and as she started to ask her question I knew what she'd ask and silently prayed for the answer I needed. She said, "If your loved one died on a cross, would you wear one around your neck?" The Spirit's answer went straight through my head to my mouth: "Yes," I replied, "if three days later he rose from the dead." Within a week she left the Witnesses and asked me to help her find a good Bible teaching church near her home.

Other cults have similar issues. Church of Christ International (COCI) believes they are the only true church of Christ. They also believe people must be baptized into their true church or they are hell bound. But they also don't believe in being reborn or Spirit filled. Ironically, though the Bible says there is no end to the increase of God's Kingdom, their 'true church' is rapidly shrinking. Why? Sixty Minutes and other main stream media outlets discovered that COCI is banned from most college campuses because of their hyper authoritarian 'evangelism and teaching'. When people convert to COCI they must submit to church authority, never use musical instruments in worship (though they were used in the Bible), stop drinking alcohol (though Jesus' first miracle turn water into wine not Welches). And if they don't do what their church leaders command, they are shamed and eventually shunned instead of lovingly restored, as Paul taught. A greater irony is that church leaders who abused women and children were not shunned, just quietly shuttled somewhere else as Catholics do with with child molesting priests. No wonder parents didn't want them talking to their college aged children.

So how do we see and receive this inner Kingdom. If we seek God until we find Him, and we welcome Jesus in, the Holy Spirit rebirths God within us just as it birthed Jesus in His mother Mary. The Holy Spirit then becomes our teacher, the Paraclete, the One who draws alongside us (and inside us) to help. (Cf. John 14:26 and other passages that label the Holy Spirit as our teacher.) God's Spirit personally teaches us what following Jesus means through His inspired Word and our own inner witness. God's Kingdom is within us because we invited Jesus into our life and made Him our King. It's among us because we are part of His Church and members of the Body of Christ which is comprised of others who also decided to follow Jesus, who alone is our way, truth and life. God dwelt in Jesus who incarnated Him to physically demonstrate what God would be like in human flesh. He was literally God with skin. The Church and each 'member' (each part of His body) can similarly reflect His physical presence to the lost world. Collectively, we're called to edify or build each other up in love using our unique gifts and calling (See Romans 12 and I Corinthians 12-13).

When I was first born again, I felt as if all of my life went from boring black and white to vibrant living color. God's

Word, which previously had been a dull lifeless tome, suddenly came alive as I earnestly sought Him. His way of living suddenly made more sense to me than anything I had ever read or heard. This occurred as soon as the eyes of my heart were opened and my spiritual blindness healed. This happened because I was in such desperate straits that I promised to do whatever His Word said. Immediately the scales fell off my eyes as I read the red letter words of Jesus in Matthew. And of course, until you can see what a wonderful things God's Kingdom is, you can't enter it; you won't even want to.

Jesus' parables make a fascinating study in and of themselves. They are short allegorical stories designed to illustrate or teach some essential truth, principle or moral lesson. Each makes a statement or commentary that conveys a meaning indirectly by the use of comparisons or analogies. Each of these extended metaphors and similes conveys a powerful meaning. The story form also gives the message more 'stickability' making it easier to remember, reflect on and assimilate.

How to Interpret Parables

If we're to properly interpret the parables, we must examine their context. Someone said "text without context is pretext" and they're right. Until we understand what the symbols in a parable meant to the people who first heard it, we can't accurately understand its personal implications for us.

One misunderstanding many people share is that most of

us believe that Jesus used parables designed to make it easier for us to comprehend. Just the opposite is true. Jesus used parables to hide the meaning of His message (Luke 8:10). Some people just wanted to use Jesus for what He could do for them immediately, with no intention of following Him. Other's understood the incredible benefit of this His new way of living and they didn't want to miss out on any of it. They became His true followers and most were probably present when the Holy Spirit fell upon the 120 or so who gathered in an upper room for the first true Pentecost (Acts 1:15-26).

William Barclay, my favorite commentator on the gospels, applied a unique scholarly genius to his relevant, simple, practical studies of the New Testament. He says "The parable conceals truth from those who are either too lazy to think or too blind through prejudice to see" (The Gospel of Matthew Volume 2, p.62). It will never make sense to scoffers. I know. I was one!

Jesus' enemies went beyond mockery: they sought to use Jesus' own words to trap Him in some supposed heresy that they could use to kill Him. However, His disciples knew He could do the most for them if they understood every word He uttered, so after the crowd thinned, they pressed him for deeper understanding (Luke 8:9). We're told that the people knew God's acts, but Moses knew God's ways (Psalm 103:7). The disciples were more like Moses, which explains how they impacted the world so profoundly. If we want to impact our world we must follow their lead and seek to know and obey everything He taught.

How did Jesus interpret His parables? He shows us when He explains the parable of the wheat and tares (cf. Matthew 13). Each symbol implied something specific: the sower is Jesus, the field is the world, the good seed are the sons of God's Kingdom and the tares represent the sons of Satan (verses 37-38). Jesus went on to explain that the enemy who sowed bad seed is the devil. The harvest represents the end of the age, and angels are the reapers. But there was still one central meaning to the parable: Jesus will eventually send his angels to gather out of His kingdom offensive people who practice lawlessness and cast then into a 'fiery furnace' where they will perish (not be tortured forever). But the righteous will shine forth as the sun in their Father's eternal Kingdom.

This pattern of interpretation, given to us by Jesus Himself, will serve us well as we examine all His parables. Each item has a symbolic meaning, but each story contains a central message.

As I said, some parables are mentioned in all three synoptic gospels, some shared in two and others in only one. However, just because something is mentioned only once, that doesn't make it less important. The mandate to be born again to see and enter His kingdom only appears in John's gospel and there may not be a more important revelation anywhere in the entire Bible.

Matthew, Mark and Luke all mention the parables of the Sower and Seed, the House Divided against Itself, the Mustard Seed, the Wicked Vine Dressers and the Fig Tree. So let's examine those first.

We've already discussed the central message of the

sower. In His imagery of a house divided against itself, Jesus answers those who accused him of using satanic power to cast out demons. He exposes the absurdity of such an assertion by pointing out that any kingdom fighting against its own interest would not be able to survive. Since the religious hypocrites also sought to cast out demons, He brilliantly turns His detractors' against themselves. He exposes His accusers false assertion by affirming that if He casts out demons using God's power then God's Kingdom has come to them through Him.

In the parable of the Mustard Seed, Barclay says "The point is crystal clear, The Kingdom of Heaven starts from the smallest beginnings, but no man knows where it will end" (IBID, Barclay, p. 85). We should never despise small beginnings. The increase of God's Kingdom will never end. Jesus does not want any to perish but for all to come to repentance (Cf. II Peter 3).

The parable of the wicked vine dressers vividly shows us how unique Jesus is in coming to save the world from the false vine dressers who wanted to use God's Kingdom for their personal profit. He reminds us that brokenness is part of the legacy of those who fall on the rock of Jesus, but those who refuse to do so suffer a worse fate: they will be crushed to dust. Perhaps only then can they ever hope to add living water and become pliable clay in the Master's hand (Matthew 21:44).

Finally, in the parable of the figs (Matthew 21 and Mark 11), Jesus demonstrates a powerful message to His astonished disciples: whatever they pray with unquestioning faith will inevitably come to pass. As with all parables, there are other messages as well. For example, fruit bearing is essential and inevitable for those who attach themselves to Jesus as their Vine (John 15).

Both Matthew and Luke cover several Kingdom parables that Mark ignores, including the Wheat and Tares, the Hidden Treasure, the Pearl of Great Price, the Dragnet, the Unforgiving Servant, Two Workers in a Vineyard, the Two Sons, the Wedding Feast and last but not least,the Parable of the Talents.

Barclay says that the Precious Pearl story tells us that the Kingdom of heaven is the loveliest thing in the world (10 IBID, Barclay, p. 97). He goes on to say that "the will of God is no grim, gray, agonizing thing. Beyond the discipline, beyond the sacrifice, beyond the self-denial, beyond the cross, there lies the supreme loveliness which is nowhere else." Ho goes on to say that there is only one way to bring peace to the heart, joy to the mind and beauty to the life, and that is to accept the will of God. "The supreme pearl is the willing obedience which makes us friends with God" (IBID., Barclay).

In my book Precious Pearls I was curious to know something:

Why did Jesus refer to a pearl instead of a diamond or other more valuable gemstone?

I discovered two astonishing reasons. First, pearls are the only gem that is organic. It comes from an inner agitation that wounds the oyster whose body creates an incredibly beautiful luminous protection against further injury from the pain. Second, the most precious gem in the world isn't a diamond or any non-organic stone that comes from inside the earth. It's a 75 pound pearl worth over one hundred million dollars! Jesus sure knew what to use in His story. Omniscience has its benefits!

The parable of the Hidden Treasure conveys a similar message but highlights the fact that in order to purchase such a great treasure we must sell everything we have and buy the whole field in which it is buried. Some say the field represents the Church; gathering together with other Christians, not forsaking fellowship, as tempting as that may be sometimes. It is worth all we own to gain this Kingdom treasure, including submitting ourselves and possessions with reckless abandon to the will of God and all that it entails, even the peculiar people who comprise His Kingdom (Titus 2:14, I Peter 2:9).

There are people today who secretly use metal detectors to examine land that's for sale where they believe there may be treasure hidden. When they find it, they buy the specific parcel they want and dig it up! Could they have gotten that idea from the Bible?

The Dragnet parable reminds us that God's 'fishing' net catches everything, good and bad, but it is God's job to judge which is which, not ours. He alone can righteously separate the good from the evil and that will only happen at the end of time.

In the parable of the Unforgiving Servant, Jesus isn't talking about money. He reminds us that if we have been forgiven for everything we've ever done wrong, who are we to harbor resentment and unforgiveness against someone who has wronged us? Ultimately, forgiveness is a gift we give ourselves; it does little if anything for the person we forgive. Someone said unforgiveness is like drinking deadly poison and expecting it to harm someone else. Selah!

In the parable of the Two Vineyard Workers, one has lived a life that's worthy of the Kingdom while one hasn't, and the consequences are enormous. The Two Sons story reminds us that there are two kinds of people, those who say yes and do no, and those who say no but do yes. Those who drag their feet are often far more productive for the Kingdom than those who say whatever we want to hear but don't honor their word. Sadly, the church is full of people who have no idea what it means to do what they say. For some reason, I find that young pastors are prone to dishonor their word in this way. Perhaps it's because their load in life and ministry is so great. In all honesty, I was like that too when

The powerful message of the Wedding Feast Parable should sober us all. Truly the good is the enemy of the best. Many who are invited to the eternal banquet are too absorbed with family, work and their own interests to care much about God's plan for their lives. None of those things are bad in themselves, but any of them can usurp the supreme position that God alone and His perfect purpose should have in our life. Each can become a perilous distraction from making the most important thing the most important thing. Perhaps this also explains why the poor are so blessed: God's Kingdom and its rewards, in this life and the next, truly do belong to them.

Finally, the famous parable of the Talents has nothing to do with money either. It reminds us that how we steward our entire life, not just our finances, determines our eternal reward. In Our Father's house are many mansions, but not all of us are guaranteed one. I know people who lived in splendid mansions in this life who will be fortunate and grateful to have a shack in the next. I remember seeing a guy in seminary who was constantly helping every person he could. I asked him why. He said he had a ministry of helps and was sending up lumber for his heavenly home!

No wonder these memorable stories became a part of the legacy of Matthew, Mark and Luke. Each one uniquely addresses common tendencies we all share; tendencies that could substantially rob us of Kingdom bliss both in this world and the next.

Kingdom Parables taught in Only One Gospel

Only Mark recounted Jesus' poignant story of the Growing Seed, but thank God he did. This parable sparkles with relevance for each of us. It reminds us that good seed – Kingdom people – bear fruit by virtue of just their contact with the soil of this world. When seed is good and it comes in contact with soil, it can't help but reproduce. This strikes to the heart of those who feel that they aren't evangelists, or they are not called to bring people to Christ. We are all called to do the work of evangelists (II Timothy 4:5). If our lives reflect Jesus' love, people will see a difference in us. Better yet, they will want to know our Lord just by rubbing up against us. I mentioned in a sermon once that we should remember LNF. People looked at me funny, then I said "Love Never Fails." One of my friends heard that and tells me LNF whenever I see him. I now end many of my letters with that instead of GBY.

Luke is the only gospel writer to tell us the parables of the Unfinished Towers and the Minas. The first story naturally reminds us to count the cost of building our lives on the Rock of Christ. This is especially challenging. Just prior to this, Jesus warned us that we must be ready if necessary to hate father, mother, siblings, spouses and even our children if they keep us from following Him. To explain this, Barclay tells the story of a famous teacher who was told, "So and so tells me he's your student." The teacher replied, "He may have attended my lectures but he was not one of my students" (Barclay, William, The Gospel of Luke, p. 198). May that never be said of those of us who seek to follow Jesus. Are our children, spouses, and extended families more important than doing God's will? Do they offer us useful excuses for remaining lukewarm (Revelations 3:16) and uncommitted? That's a serious question for us all.

The parable of the Minas is similar to the parable of the Talents except more harsh. Let's hope Jesus was using hyperbole when he tells us the reaction of the ruler who entrusted a sum of money to a servant who did nothing with it. Upon learning this, the ruler said, "To everyone who has will be given more; and from him who has not, even what he has shall be taken away. But bring here those enemies of mine, who did not want me to rule over them, and slay them before me" (Luke 19:26-27). Have no fear, the story is based on a real event that was familiar to the people of Jesus' day when certain Jews told Augustus they did not want him to rule over them. He ordered them all slain. The point, however, is clear. We have been given one life. We must invest it wisely, not only to learn life's lessons, but also to expand our Master's Kingdom reign. Unfortunately, when I ask Christians how many people they discipled I'm usually met with a pregnant pause. Most then change the subject.

This is why I call our ministry One Life Ministries or OLM. One Life, YOUR Life Can Make a Difference. Our purpose is to help you and the whole Church have what you need to heal and disciple the nations. We are constantly developing new tools like this book, audio books, video courses and even live events and feature films to that end. You can learn more at www.SoulDr.com .

Though none of John's three parables discuss the Kingdom they are all important. Like Jesus' other parables that don't explicitly mention God's Kingdom but they all clearly teach some unique aspect of what it means to be God's children and siblings of the King of kings. Mostly they remind us that the Kingdom of God is the kingdom of right relationships. We could call them sandbox 101 for God's children.

Jesus replied, "No one who puts his hand to the plow and looks back is fit for service in the kingdom of God." - Luke 9:62

> *"And whatever we ask we receive from Him, because we keep His commandments and do the things that are pleasing in His site. And this is His commandment, that we believe in the name of His Son Jesus Christ, and love one another, just as He commands us. And the one who keeps His commandments abides in Him, and He in him. And we know by this that He abides in us, by the Spirit whom He has given us"._ I John 3:22-24*

DISCUSSION QUESTIONS

Of the parables we've just considered, which is your favorite? Why?

____

____

____

Which one scares you the most? Why?

____

____

____

Which would require the most change in your life? How would it change?

____

____

____

CHAPTER THIRTEEN

THE ETERNAL KINGDOM: DON'T RUPTURE THE RAPTURE

"I tell you the truth, some who are standing here will not taste death before they see the kingdom of God" (Luke 9:27).

"Once, having been asked by the Pharisees when the kingdom of God would come, Jesus replied, "The kingdom of God does not come with your careful observation... nor will people say, 'Here it is,' or 'there it is,' because the kingdom of God is within you" (Luke 17:20-21).

THEOLOGIANS ARGUE WHETHER GOD'S KINGDOM is reigning now on earth within us or later forever in heaven. ***Secret alert: it's both. There's an eternal Kingdom and an internal Kingdom and the two are interdependent.*** Unless He reigns within us, we won't reign with Him either in this life (Romans 5:17) or the next (Revelations 20:6). Will we get to heaven? Probably (cf. I Corinthians 3:15). Will we be glad we did? Of course. But the essence of our eternal reward and our role throughout eternity may well be impacted by how well we follow Him as our Lord in this life. That's far more essential than whether we've broken a few bad habits or believed the right doctrines. Someone once told me the devil believes in the Apostle's creed; he knows it's true, but that doesn't guarantee him a mansion in heaven. Don't be surprised if many prostitutes and alcoholics today just as in Jesus' day have a greater eternal reward than modern day Scribes and Pharisees (Matthew 21:31-2). And make no mistake; the Church has always had its share of all four.

As you've seen from the scriptures, our eternal destiny is affected by our fruitfulness (cf. John 15), our righteousness (I John 3:7), and most of all how well we have learned to love (Matthew 25). Keeping the law won't save us. No matter what Wesley believed, no one can perfectly do that (Galatians 2:16). But Luther didn't get it totally right either: faith alone can't save us (James 2:14-20). Without works is dead (verse 20). We need a fervent passionate effectual faith to live as God intends. Without righteousness, without living a loving, compassionate life, our 'faith' alone just won't work (pun intended). We also need to do the good works He created us to do (Ephesians 2:8-10)! That's a sobering thought, especially if you were indoctrinated into liberal or fundamentalist belief systems and never studied the Bible for yourself. ***Perhaps the greatest divine paradox is that not only are we chosen and have free will, but we need faith that also believes works.*** Some theologian said we must believe as if only our faith in Christ can save us and work as if it all depends on us!

=This is much bigger than an illogical paradox. Here's how our Lord helped me resolve this when I was in seminary. Calvinist Presbyterian and Wesleyan Aminian students loved to argue over free will or predestination. I was one of the few who understood that the Bible teaches both. As I prayerfully meandered through the seminary library seeking a way to resolve this debate, I was led to a book that mentioned 'thought forms'. It said that each culture has its own way of thinking. Western Greek thought demands objective intellectual consistency, while Eastern Asian thought is more subjective, emotional and heart centered. It has no problem with contradictory logic.

How did the author resolve this truth in tension? Remarkably, he said the Hebrew Bible is a middle eastern book. Consequently, both thought forms are equally honored. And isn't this what we would expect for a faith that's relevant to the entire world? For scriptural Christians, there is a time for everything, just like Ecclesiastes 3:1-8 says. It was quoted almost verbatim with some lyrical rearrangement by rock legend Pete Seeger in the beautiful song made famous by the classic rock band The Seekers in 1966.

Turn! Turn! Turn!
To everything turn turn turn
There is a season turn turn turn
And a time for every purpose under heaven
A time to be born a time to die
A time to plant a time to reap
A time to kill a time to heal
A time to laugh a time to weep

To everything turn turn turn
There is a season turn turn turn
And a time for every purpose under heaven

A time to build up a time to break down
A time to dance a time to mourn
And a time to cast away stones a time to gather stones together

To everything turn turn turn
There is a season turn turn turn
And a time for every purpose under heaven

A time of love a time of hate
A time of war a time of peace
And a time you may embrace, a time to refrain from embracing

To everything turn turn turn
There is a season turn turn turn
And a time for every purpose under heaven

A time to gain a time to lose
A time to rend a time to sew
A time to love a time to hate
A time for peace I swear it's not too late

To everything turn turn turn
There is a season turn turn turn
And a time for every purpose under heaven

Isn't that just too cool! No scriptural passage better reveals the necessity of a biblical thought form than this awesome text, believed by many to be first written by King Solomon in the tenth century BC.

But before we even get to 'eternity', there are other things we must consider. It's entirely possible, no, likely, that we are living in the last days, however we interpret the word 'day'. (Is it 24 hours or a thousand years?) Our study of God's Kingdom is incomplete unless we revisit *eschatology* – the knowledge and study of the end times. When we do that, especially in America, we may be in for some unpleasant surprises.

In addition to the failure to stress the importance of seeking first God's Kingdom and righteousness, two other things have almost paralyzed today's Church. Both flow from unbiblical doctrines that dominate the American Church. The first proceeds from an unbalanced emphasis on predestination and sovereignty and concerns the doctrine of omniscience. The second pertains to the uniquely modern American belief in a pretribulation rapture.

Okay, I know this will be controversial, but first I want to challenge some assumptions you may have made about omniscience. God certainly knows everything that exists and happens, even down to the number of hairs on our head and the sparrows that fall from the sky (Matthew 10:30). ***But what if He doesn't know everything people will do?*** If we don't have a balanced biblical theology that gives equal weight to God's sovereignty and man's free will, we may need to re-examine our definition of omniscience. If we take that doctrine further than God intended, it can lead to apathy, and that could have terrible eternal and internal consequences. As Michael Murdock says, "If God is in charge of everything, why do we punish rapists and murderers?"

As we've seen, apathy is a major problem for the American Church. Too often we're like the young man who was asked how he felt about the fact that apathy and ignorance were destroying our country. He simply said, "I don't know and I don't care."

If we believe that God has every event in history planned out and we can just 'leave it all in His hands', we will act very differently than if we recognize that God uses people to impact the course of history. The Bible and Church history are packed with individuals and groups who have done exactly that: profoundly affecting the direction and history of the world. You can probably name a handful without giving it much thought. Think of the impact of King David or Joseph in the Old Testament, or the Apostle John and Saul of Tarsus in the New. What about Martin

Luther, William Tyndale or John Wesley? It's been said that the Wesleyan revivals did for England what the French Revolution did for France only without the bloodshed. And without Luther, almost all of us would be Roman Catholics. If it weren't for Tyndale, most of the world would not be able to read the Bible in their own language.

If we believe that God ordained each of us to do certain things but, like Jesus in the Garden of Gethsemane, we always have the option of saying no, then we just might take life a lot more seriously. We might even ask God to show us what we can do to stand up for good and against evil. Edmund Burke's memorable statement that *"The only thing necessary for evil to triumph is for good men to remain silent"* may prod us out of our lethargy long enough to take action, or at least speak up! In the words of evangelist Bill Bright, we might even "come help save the world."

If the sleeping giant that is the Church awakens, no evil can triumph. The Church is the only demographic group big and influential and spiritually powerful enough to bring our nation and world back from the precipice of destruction. It was certainly so in the Great Awakenings of the past. May it be so for us again today.

If we fail at that, it's entirely possible that the worst persecution in the history of the world may knock on your door.

Which brings me to my next point: another factor that has rocked us to sleep when it should have rocked our world awake is the large number of people who either believe that the end time prophecies have already happened (many modernist theologians) or those who believe that the tribulation will never touch us (many US fundamentalists).

Liberals struggle with any literal interpretation of scripture. But there are also some real problems for fundamentalist who claim to accept the plenary (all-encompassing) inspiration of scripture. To introduce this topic, I must say that the pre-tribulation rapture theory is largely an American belief. Try telling Chinese, Russian, Indian, Middle Eastern, African or even European Christians that they won't experience tribulation. A friend just returned from India where he filmed the destruction of two hundred churches that were recently burned down. Another friend in Liberia remembers when the same thing was done there. Perhaps we Americans can only hold on to this rather recent doctrinal position because we've never been attacked or persecuted in our homeland.

Don't get me wrong, I'd love to believe we'll all get beamed up before the real shooting starts. And there are scriptural ways to avoid the Great Tribulation. But if we're not careful we may miss the fact that the conditions for that are not as simple as most think. So let's dive in and resolve this.

The Bible clearly teaches that Great Tribulation precedes Jesus' return for us. All three synoptic gospels agree on this. (Read Matthew 24 Mark 13 and Luke 21 carefully, noting the precise sequence of events). As I alluded to earlier, I fear that many who have been taught that all Christians will escape the Great Tribulation will turn away from and even against Christians if they find out that they too must go through Tribulation. ***Remember, we do through much tribulation enter into God's Kingdom (Acts 14:22).*** Those who expect to get there any other way could be the very people who comprise the great falling away that the New Testament talks about (II Thessalonians 2:3). In their bitterness, rage and disappointment they could incite the persecution of Christians.

One thing's certain: if we believe that the forces of hell on earth could assault us and our loved ones once satanically inspired people gain power and influence, we will act very differently than if we believe that all that hatred will be directed against Jews after we're gone. I hope I'm wrong about this. I've been wrong at least three times in my life when I thought I understood the end times. Smart Christians have erred on this for almost 2,000 years. But at the very least, let's open our Bibles for some serious research on the end times. God plus one is a majority. We can each make a real difference, but only if we stay awake and not asleep, as the Bible warns (I Thessalonians 5:1-8).

When the Kingdom Comes

Why do some believe that the pretrib rapture doctrine is the greatest threat to the Church today? To answer this question, let's explore the checkered history of the 'Pretrib' doctrine.

First, here's a short primer on *Hermeneutics* (the responsible practice of biblical interpretation). Whenever we interpret scripture, a threefold test should be used to understand the true meaning of a passage. This methodology is called the Historical, Grammatical and Theological Hermeneutic.

When we examine Church history and the birth of the pretrib doctrine, we discover that at no time in history or any geographical place where Christianity developed was this doctrine taught until 19th century America. It was popularized in an 1830 prophecy given by 15 year old Margaret McDonald. Before that J.N. Darby, a devious religious attorney, unsuccessfully tried to promote it. The doctrine, which is established on the shifting sand of symbols, inferences and metaphors, is not based on rock solid literal scripture. The rationales they developed contradict clear Bible teaching. But Darby and others were so clever, they actually revised the Reformer's hymns to make it appear that they believed it too.

The most basic principle of Hermeneutics is that a clear teaching of Scripture can only be ignored or refuted when another clear teaching from Scripture contradicts and supersedes it. An example of this is the way in which the New Testament doctrine proclaiming all foods acceptable supplants Old Testament about eating pork. As an intriguing aside, Jesus also issued about 70 commandments, not just the two great ones. A simple web search details them.

Scofield and Ryrie both developed study Bibles that included pretrib rapture notes. Scofield was eventually jailed as a forger while Ryrie was later plagiarized by author Hal Lyndsey. Both their Bibles and Lyndsey's writings were extremely popular during the Jesus movement when new Christians distrusted churches and hungered for a simple explanation of the Bible.

A fundamentalist novelist sold millions of books to those who learned their eschatology from him. One researcher, whose name eludes me said, "It started with *The Late Great Planet Earth* and continues with the *Left Behind* series, novels on prophecy and the end-times that enthralled naive conservative Christians. Never mind that most of the things in these books (except the Second Coming of Christ) will never take place. They are based on faulty interpretations of Scripture." That's how in ***Left Behind: Separating Fact From Fiction***, Gary DeMar "brilliantly skewers all the pretentious prophecy claims, shows there's no biblical support, and returns sanity to Christian hopes for the future" according to Paul Maier, Professor of Ancient History and bestselling author of the novel ***Skeleton in God's Closet***.

Who wouldn't love to believe we must do nothing but say the sinner's prayer in order to escape the Great Tribulation? Many pastors who got swept into the ministry from the Jesus movement distrusted religious authority so they didn't get a seminary degree. Many never studied Greek, Hebrew, Biblical Theology, Systematic Theology or Hermeneutics. Consequently very few do adequate background research into church history to see which reputable and respected scholars researched and taught certain doctrines. Many never attained the tools that enable them to analyze the original languages. Most have no framework for distinguishing between true scriptural hermeneutics and overly simplistic misleading ones.

One Seminary made the pretrib rapture the hallmark of their eschatology. The doctrine was so popular that Jesus movement baby boomers were more likely to attend there than other seminaries. I'm told that the President of that institution twisted the scholarship of Robert Gundry to support his pretrib position. He later refused to respond to a 35 page document refuting it.

Again, no other country but the US and no era or segment of Christianity (Catholicism, Greek, Russian or Eastern Orthodox, etc.) throughout church history has embraced the pretrib rapture. That's not because of new information, it's because the doctrine is rebutted by scripture in Matthew 24 and Mark 13. Notice the sequence of events those gospels describe: ***"But immediately after the tribulation of those days the sun will be darkened and the moon will not give its light and the stars will fall from the sky and the powers of the heavens will be shaken, and then the sign of the Son of Man will appear in the sky, and then all the tribes of the earth will mourn, and they will see the Son of Man coming on the clouds of the sky with power and great glory. And he will send forth His angels with a great trumpet and they will gather together the elect from the four winds, from that end of the sky to the other" (Matthew 24:29-32). "For those days will be a time of tribulation such as has not occurred since the beginning of the creation which God created, until now,***

and never shall. And unless the Lord had shortened those days, no life would have been saved; but for the sake of the elect whom he chose, he shortened those days"(Mark 13:19-20). "But in those days, after the tribulation, the sun will be darkened, and the moon will not give its light, and the stars will be falling from heaven, and the powers that are in the heavens will be shaken. And then they will see the Son of Man coming in clouds with great power and glory. And then he will send forth the Angels and would gather together his elect from the four winds, from the farthest end of the earth to the farthest end of heaven" (Vss. 24-27).

The last I knew, the largest Pentecostal denomination in the world still teaches pretrib rapture, but at the time the decision was made to accept it they reportedly had as many dissenters as not, but "the pretrib followers shouted louder".

People who embrace pretrib doctrine usually say, "God won't take out his wrath on Christians," but the Bible clearly teaches that the tribulation isn't God's wrath, it is Satan's. God's wrath is clearly visited on the earth after the tribulation (Cf. Matthew 24:29 and Revelations 6.)

More Problems with the Pretrib Doctrine

A. It must redefine the biblical teaching of Election in order to make a radical distinction between Jews and Christians. Election is used only 4 times in the OT, referring to Jews, and 21 times in the NT where it always refers to Christians. Yet proponents of pretrib doctrine insists at some points in the NT it means Jews and at other points it means Christians. They offer no scriptural proof for their argument. They have none.

B. Instead of being based on solid exegesis (extracting from scripture what's in it) it requires much eisegesis (reading into scripture what isn't there). This sort of "private interpretation of scripture" is directly condemned by the Bible (II Peter 1:20-21). It's more terrifying if it's done to the book of Revelations (Cf Revelations 22:18-19).

C. In II Thessalonians 2, "that which restrains" never says it's the Holy Spirit in believers that restrains evil, which must be believed if the doctrine is to hold up under scrutiny. That which restrains could just as easily mean current attempts to drive Christianity from the public square, the erosion of the influence of Christianity on behavior, values and ethics, or the falling away of Christians. **Again, wherever the Bible explicitly teaches something, the mere interpretation of prophetic inferences and eisegesis are never sufficient to repudiate it.** Scripture can only be abrogated by another scripture that explicitly displaces it.

D. Twisting and distorting scriptures to deceive the untaught instead of plainly accepting scripture at face value is clearly condemned in the NT. Peter warned against this: II Peter 3:9-18.

E. Dangers:

1. Presumption that leads to deception forms false teaching. We are constantly warned against false teachers using deception in the last days related to the coming of

Christ. (Mark 13, Matthew 24, Luke 21, etc.) Presumptuous sin is the worst consequence of this deception, and presuming on God's love, grace, mercy and compassion leads to most if not all insidious sins and iniquities.

2. Apathy about the world, not doing what God puts us here to do, and assuming we are saved when a person may not even have been born again, are the terrible consequences of being half-hearted. I need not remind you what happens to the lukewarm.

The only way to escape the great tribulation? Pray, Watch and Be Accounted Worthy (Luke 21).

This means being "righteous as Jesus was righteous." I call this Realized Righteousness, not just trusting *imputed righteousness*. When Jesus returns, it's for people who are busy doing their father's business, not religious busy bodies squandering their lives.

Dietrich Bonhoeffer said "The sin of respectable people reveals itself in flight from responsibility." He also said we must not only care for the victims of reckless drivers but make sure that such people can't get behind the wheel of a car. He was talking about much more than Mothers Against Drunk Driving. When he said this about apathetic Christians who never resisted the likes of Adolf Hitler who later arrested and condemned Bonhoeffer, He put his money where his mouth was. He was executed by the Nazis just before the end of World War II.

Sadly, most Christian leaders today ignore the clear

mandate of scripture to "rule in this world" (Romans 5:17), choosing instead to avoid messy political stuff that might offend someone. They too often shun their scriptural responsibility to help get the righteous into power so the world can rejoice Cf. Proverbs 25:26). Instead they presume we won't even be here when the dung hits the fan, so why bother with those who will be left behind!

The Biblical Basis for Mid or Post-Trib

A. Matthew 24 isn't just for Jews it's for disciples. Not all of Jesus disciples were Jews.

B. All three synoptic gospels teach mid or post-trib. Even if we assume Matthew was addressing Jews, Mark 13 parallels Matthew 24, and teaches the same thing. If we ignore everything Jesus taught to Jews we must ignore most of what Jesus taught. The only Bible He had was the Old Testament and he quoted it 78 times.

C. Luke 21 doesn't negate the relevance of the Mark or Matthew's Olivet discourses. In all three Jesus answer questions from His disciples about the end time. Luke tells us to "keep on the alert at all times, praying in order that you may have strength to escape all these things that are about to take place, and to stand before the Son of Man" (Luke 21:36). Matthew 25 adds to this ***DOING*** the works Jesus did, as does John 14:12. And the book of Revelations teaches over and over that we must all endure to the end.

D. Having said 1 that, it's possible some who are raptured will go in the middle, some at the end, others obviously can die beforehand or endure. This would hinge on where they live and what they are doing when Jesus returns. In recent years, people under the evil religious demonic rage of ISIS would never tell you they did not experience Great Tribulation. ***Watch, pray, and act. This is the only biblically guaranteed way to escape Tribulation.*** Just asking Jesus to be your Savior won't do it, unless you're the thief on the cross, or make Him your Lord and die before you demonstrate your fidelity to Him.

Authentic disciples do the works Jesus did and greater(John 14:12). They also obey all that He taught (Cf. Mark 16, Mt. 28). ***True disciples seek to make more disciples by teaching them to obey all that Jesus taught (John 15, etc.).*** (Again, a simple web search lists all Jesus's commands.)

E. In Jesus' prayer for all who would follow Him He said: I pray not that thou shouldest take them out of the world, but that thou shouldest keep them from evil. In Rev. 3:10 Apostle John tells us that those who "have kept my command to endure patiently, ***I will also keep you from the hour of trial that is going to come on the whole world to test the inhabitants of the earth."***

Summary: pre-trib rapture doctrine as it's usually taught is such a great threat to God's Kingdom because:

1. First it's based on half-truths, bad theology and distortions, the very deceptions Jesus warned us about in the last days.

2. Mark 13 and Matthew 24 clearly teach great tribulation before Jesus returns for us.

3. Using elaborate theological schemes to ignore the simple clear meaning of scripture is forbidden and warned against. There is no private interpretation of scripture (II Peter 3:9-18).

4. Pretrib leads to presumption, creating a lazy lukewarm church that doesn't do God's work or seek to reign in this life (Cf. Psalm 19:13, Revelations 3) or do the works Jesus did. Sadly, many believers have never made one disciple and that's why God redeemed us: to be fruitful and multiply. He gave all of us the ministry of reconciling sinners to Him. The Great Commission is the call of every true disciple (numerous scriptures like Matt. 28:18-20, Mk. 16:14-20, Romans 5:11, etc.).

5. Pretrib leads people to believe they will escape suffering when Jesus and Paul call us to participate in the fellowship of Christ's suffering (I Peter 4:13 and elsewhere). Jesus prayed not that His people would escape evil but that they would endure it(John 17).

6. It could spawn the huge end-time falling away as people rush to renounce Christ rather than face persecution.

7. Those who have been deceived will not only be unprepared for tribulation, but they also might even encourage persecution of Christians because they've been lied to.

8. Ponder this: "God Himself will send a strong delusion causing condemnation on those who didn't believe the truth but had pleasure in unrighteousness" (II Thes.2:11-12). Unless we "receive the love of the truth," we will be deceived (II Thes. 2:10). God's Word is truth (John 17).

9. Pastors ignore the mandate to teach people to reign in life (Cf. Romans 5), leaving our political system to corrupt liars and thieves instead of creating a nation where the people rejoice because the righteous rule. NOTE: Our constitution doesn't mandate the separation of church and state, the old Soviet Union's did.

10. Apathy towards a needy world can get us cast into outer darkness (Matt. 24-25).I know two people who have been there and I would NOT want to spend eternity there!

Study, Watch, Pray, Persevere and Obey. That's our only true hope of escaping tribulation. Asking Jesus to become your savior and telling him you believe He's God won't buy you a cheap ticket to heaven; only allowing Him to be your King will do that. ***You must be born again. You must die to yourself and live for Him.***

As a young Christian, I led many to the Lord and even before I became a pastor I baptized them. In Ohio when we had no swimming pool or baptism font, we'd break the ice on Lake Erie if necessary to baptize people. I instructed them in the scriptural meaning of baptism and told them I'd be asking them if they are

willing to live and died for Jesus. Only then would I perform their baptism (obviously by immersion). Most who were so instructed and baptized in that fashion went on to serve the Lord full time. One that I know of started and pastored a huge megachurch. Two others started prison ministries that discipled untold thousands to follow Jesus in all US prison and eight other nations. When we do things God's way, our fruit multiplies and remains.

DISCUSSION QUESTIONS

Does this chapter change your understanding of the timing of the Rapture?

____

____

____

____

How do you feel about that?

____

____

____

Are you watching, praying, persevering and becoming worthy by doing your Father's business? How?

____

____

____

CHAPTER FOURTEEN

WHAT CAN STEAL YOUR INHERITANCE?

ONE LAST MAJOR CONCERN: if the gospel of the Kingdom of God is His greatest bequest to us, we must be aware of something essential that few Christians realize. Certain transgressions if we refuse to renounce them, can hinder our entire inheritance.

Contrary to what you may have been told, all sins are not created equal. Some can cause us eternal regret (I John 5:16-17). We must carefully consider the passages that warn us of those and, in the poignant words of a wise old preacher: 'If the shoe fits don't go home barefoot'.

There are far more than seven deadly sins. In my first best selling book *True Sexuality*, I listed the handful of verses that compile them. See for yourself. They include Romans 1:29-32, I Corinthians 6:9-10, II Corinthians 12:20-21, Galatians 5:19-21, and Revelations 21:7-8. Naturally they list the 24 conventional carnal sins: adultery, murder, theft, violence, sexual immorality, wickedness, drunkenness, revelries, covetousness, evil-mindedness, sorcery, licentiousness and heresy. Let's call those the sins of the flesh. But they also include more than twice as many other serious iniquities that we might not suspect. This list of 29 grave sins involves what I call sins of the spirit. Most are relational transgressions against God and people like lying, envy, jealousy, extortion, selfish ambition, unbelief, dissension, contentions, cowardice, outbursts of wrath, deceit, conceit, pride, unrighteousness, back-biting, gossip, variance (causing division), reviling, maliciousness, tumultuousness, inventors of evil, haters of God, idolatry, untrustworthiness, disobedience to parents as well as being unloving, unforgiving and unmerciful. Whew, that's quite a comprehensive catalog.

Sins of the flesh mostly hurt the sinner, but sins of the spirit usually devastate others as well. The first group of sins we would expect to find in any compilation of personal vices. We aren't surprised to see them in what some call 'worldly' people, or 'carnal Christians' who may have never experienced a palpable encounter with God's love. However, George Barna's surveys show that these sins affect a significant part of contemporary churchianity.

Sadly, people guilty of the sins of the spirit may also occupy high places in churches and denominations, such as church boards and commissions. When I was in the evangelical Good News movement of the United Methodist Church, an executive from IBM who had been in denominational meetings at the highest level, said he saw things there that would make secular corporate executives blush.

It's easy for us to tee off on what we may call sins of the

flesh, quite another thing to preach against the kind of behavior we readily tolerate and almost celebrate in some religious circles. Selfish ambition, jealousy, gossip, pride, variance, tumults and self-righteousness can contaminate the quality of fellowship in churches and sully the spiritual atmosphere enough to make it toxic.

There are people in churches who have never had sex outside of marriage who are guilty of spiritual adultery. Perhaps that's because money, power, control and idolatry are their lords, not Jesus Christ.

Do you think I'm exaggerating? Statistics on problems in the American church are staggering, especially as they impact the clergy. Years ago, H. B. London of Focus on the Family said in *Pastors In Crisis* that 80% of pastors believe the ministry affects their families negatively, 48% say it's an outright hazard to their family; 45% report depression or burnout so severe they had to take a leave of absence from pastoral ministry; ***75% report a significant stress related crisis at least once a year in their ministry; 40% report a serious conflict with a parishioner at least once a month***; 19% say they have been forced out of ministry at least once. I doubt that things have improved since those studies.

No wonder clergy have the one of the highest divorce rates of any profession. Small wonder that almost half of pastor's wives take anti-depressants. The situation is so bad that in Canada they defined 'pastoral abuse' as a special disorder that requires uniquely targeted treatment.

In the first church I pastored, my young wife contracted colitis as a result of the toxic attitudes in the women's society. It was so bad the doctors considered surgery. Within a month of my resigning from that church her symptoms totally disappeared!

On another matter, perhaps nothing is more mood altering than self- righteousness. That's why religious addiction may be the worst compulsion in America. It even afflicts 'nonreligious' people. Have you ever been to a PETA meeting, or listened as atheists rail against Christians or liberals against conservatives and vice versa? No wonder our own self- righteousness is as menstrous rags in God's sight (Isaiah 64:6). I don't mean to be offensive but the Bible doesn't mince words. This is the real meaning of the passage translated filthy rags in Isaiah 64:6. Such rags were the worst kind of personal uncleanness to ancient Jews. Women weren't even allowed to even dwell in the community during that time of month. *Imagine someone proudly cloaked in menstrous rags as their personal garment of righteousness.*

Our 'righteous indignation' causes terrible suffering in families, churches and society at large. It's understandable why those who gossip, whisper, and cause dissension, contentions, outbursts of wrath, deceit, conceit, pride, unrighteousness, back-biting, reviling, maliciousness, and evil inventions are banished from God's Kingdom. ***Heaven wouldn't be heavenly if it were populated with people like that.***

These toxic attitudes start with people who never dealt with their own bitterness, unforgiveness and unloving attitudes (Hebrews 12:15). Instead of facing these inner issues they project them onto their imperfect pastor, the pastor's family and others who disagree with them and threaten their control.

A woman once told me her marriage fell apart when she became 'charismatic' in her worship. For years they had attended a famous fundamental church in southern California. The pastor has a national radio ministry in which he openly assaults those who believe in spiritual gifts. When she began speaking in tongues her husband became hostile and cruel, eventually driving her out of her own home. After she left the church she realized most of the people there were judgmental and many were outright mean. They don't call 'em fightin' fundies for nothing. After speaking with people who knew that famous pastor very well, I concluded it's much worse than some cults.

Perhaps we should root out those kinds of people from the Church before we worry so much about wine bibbers and adulterers. That's called a back door revival. The theory is that if you drive out the trouble makers the church can grow healthy again. Control freaks can ruin God's people and reputation quicker than immoral people any day. ***The tongue is a dangerous instrument, right? It harms far more people than promiscuity ever could.***

I'm not pointing fingers here. When Jesus said if we lust after a woman we're guilty of adultery and if we're angry at a brother without a cause we have committed murder, he didn't leave any of us much wiggle room. But lest we all feel overwhelmed and hopeless in the light of these abominable sins, let's remember that verb tenses are important and not always obvious in our English Bible. We all sin and fall short of God's glory (Romans 3:23). But scriptures are clear that whether our favorite addiction is booze, broads or bad behavior in board rooms, if we ***practice*** these sins, we will not inherit Kingdom bliss in this life and we may even jeopardize it in the next. I used to joke that I don't need to practice sin; it comes quite easy to me, I'm a natural born sinner!

Those who honestly struggle with any sin are not automatically condemned just because so far they just have not yet learned how to conquer it. As long as they confess, God freely forgives them (I John 1:9). But those who justify their bad behavior are another story. It's the difference between ***sin and Iniquity***. The first means falling short of living gloriously, the later is intentional evil acts and not even trying to stop wickedness, evil doing, immorality or unfair behavior.

Thankfully, God doesn't judge us on outer appearances like people do; He looks on our heart (I Samuel 16:7). As soon as I discovered God cared more about my intentions than my performance, I finally started to comprehend the magnitude of God's great grace and mercy (*lovingkindness*). If we acknowledge our sinful tendencies and sincerely desire to be rid of them, He can heal our inner wounds and free us from their tyranny (Cf. Jeremiah 30). It's only if we rationalize and practice bad behavior that we are in danger of forfeiting our eternal inheritance.

Remember, on a more positive not, we can ***"be of good cheer, little children, it's your Father's good pleasure to give you His kingdom***" (Luke 12:32). He longs to give you His Kingdom. As we've seen, it contains everything you could ever want in this life and the next. That's the great good news of the Kingdom of Heaven. See why it's the best news in the universe? We need it and our friends, family and neighbors need it. The whole world needs it. The whole world craves it. Let's first get it for ourselves so we can pass it on. I can't think of anything better to live for, can you?

"For in those days there will be tribulation, such as has not been from the beginning of creation until this time, nor shall ever be. And unless the Lord had shortened those days, no flesh would be saved; but for the elect's sake, whom He chose, He shortened those days. But in those days, after that tribulation, the sun will be darkened, and the moon will not give its light; the stars of heaven will fall, and the powers of heaven will be shaken. Then they will see the Son of Man coming in the clouds with great power and glory. And then He will send His angels, and gather together His elect from the four winds, from the farthest part of the earth to the farthest part of heaven." – Mark 13:19-20, 24-27.

THAT'S the real rapture. Behold this glorious contrast:

> *"Now the works of the flesh are evident, which are: adultery, fornication, uncleanness, licentiousness, idolatry, sorcery, hatred, contentions, jealousies, outbursts of wrath, selfish ambitions, dissensions, heresies, envy, murders, drunkenness, revelries, and the like: of which I tell you beforehand, just as I also told you in time past, that those who practice such things will not inherit the kingdom of God. But the fruit of the Spirit is*

love, joy, peace, patience, kindness, goodness, faithfulness, gentleness, self-control. Against such there is no law." - Galatians 5:19-23

"Not everyone who says to Me, 'Lord, Lord, shall enter the kingdom of heaven, but he who does the will of My Father in heaven." - Matthew 7:21

DISCUSSION QUESTIONS

What is the eternal Kingdom Jesus talked about?

____

____

____

____

Which deadly sins surprised you?

____

____

____

____

Of the 43 deadly sins mentioned in this chapter, which ones are hardest to understand?

____

____

____

____

CHAPTER FIFTEEN

THE GREATEST NEW WORLD ORDER: GOD'S KINGDOM

Jesus won't return until the gospel of God's Kingdom is proclaimed in every nation.

LORD WILLING, WE WILL SOON LAUNCH Spiritual Awakening events we call the Kingdom Tsunami. We'll use music to draw the crowds along with a Kingdom message and hands-on healing of broken hearts and bodies to encourage people to fully surrender their lives to Jesus. It is based on the end time promises of Jeremiah 30 which empowers God's people to demonstrate and proclaim the reign of God's Kingdom to the ends of the earth. No one is talking about this but the whole global Church needs it. You can learn more about it at www.SoulDr.com .

As I've shown you, Jesus' only gospel was the awesome great news of God's Heavenly Kingdom, "on earth as it is in heaven." How can this be? Jeremiah 30 explains exactly the way it will happen in the latter days and what glorious consequences will flow from it, on earth as it is in Heaven.

I pray you find great encouragement as we consider Jeremiah's prophecy in detail. You'll see that when God heals the pain of His people, incredible blessings will erupt and create a spiritual flood of life across the entire earth. In the latter days we will finally understand this and see it come to pass. In fact, we His people will become free and healthy enough to hasten it. Let's explore Jeremiah 30 and see why this is necessary.

Instead of terrifying tribulation, God offers us an incomparable message of hope and victory.

Jeremiah 30:3 "For behold, days are coming,' declares the LORD, 'when I will restore the fortunes of My people Israel and Judah.' The LORD says, I will also bring them back to the land that I gave to their forefathers and they shall possess it." I believe this began in 1948, when Israel became a nation. It accelerated in 1967 when Jews occupied Judea for the first time in centuries.

Verses 30:4-7: "Now these are the words which the LORD spoke concerning Israel and concerning Judah: For thus says the LORD, 'I have heard a sound of terror, of dread, and there is no peace. Ask now, and see if a male can give birth. Why do I see every man {with} his hands on his loins, as a woman in childbirth? And {why} have all faces turned pale? Alas! for that day is great, there is none like it; And it is the time of Jacob's distress, but he will be saved from it." (Transgender-ism anyone?)

The holocaust of Nazi persecution preceded the establishment of the nation of Israel. But I don't for a minute believe that Jeremiah's prophecy only pertains to Jews. We can also see in our own day the satanic New World Order's attempt to destroy families, the building block of society, through the sexual revolution, feminism, and gender dysphoria. It's already taken a severe toll. In 1970, 71% of young women were married; today only 40%. In addition to that,41% of transgenders commit suicide and 80% attempt it. Many students lose their faith during college. These things have hastened the decimation of our whole culture and caused most people terrible heartbreak and misery. It's gotten so bad that the **DSM (Diagnostic and Statistical Manual of Mental Disorders) has a new category of diagnosis: *Broken Heart Syndrome.* But without God, drugs can't cure it.** Like most western medicine they only treat the symptoms.

Verses 30:8-9: `It shall come about on that day,' declares the LORD of hosts, `that I will break his yoke from off their neck and will tear off their bonds; and strangers will no longer make them their slaves. 'But they shall serve the LORD their God and David their king, whom I will raise up for them."

I've been told that even noted Israeli rabbis are beginning to acknowledge that Jesus is the Messiah.

Verses 30:10-11: `Fear not, O Jacob My servant,' declares the LORD, `and do not be dismayed, O Israel; for behold, I will save you from afar and your offspring from the land of their captivity. And Jacob will return and will be quiet and at ease, and no one will make him afraid. For I am with you,' declares the LORD, `to save you; for I will destroy completely all the nations where I have scattered you, only I will not destroy you completely. But I will chasten you justly and will by no means leave you unpunished.'

Is Armageddon's coming next?

Verses 30:12-13: "For thus says the LORD, `Your wound is incurable and your injury is serious. There is no one to plead your cause; {No} healing for {your} sore, no recovery for you."

Another translation says there is no medicine to heal you. A pharmacology professor admitted to me that pharmaceuticals can't cure anything and always have side effects, some of which are worse than the disease they treat. The root word for pharmaceutical is *pharmakia*: witchcraft; using potions to treat diseases.

In researching my book, *TRANSFORMATIONAL HEALING*, I learned that addiction recovery fails 81% of the time and costs almost $30,000 per month. When a Christian psychiatrist saw the powerful results of Transformational Healing (which I explain in my healing books), he said it's the missing piece to recovery. He said he knew that emotional pain caused addiction, but through my Transformational Healing Seminar he finally saw it cured. ***And it's all based on God's promises to heal His people's pain in the end times.***

Verses 30:14-15: `All your lovers have forgotten you, they do not seek you; for I have wounded you with the wound of an enemy, with the punishment of a cruel one, because your *iniquity* is great {And} your sins are numerous. Why do you cry out over your injury? Your pain is incurable, because your iniquity is great, your sins are numerous. I have done these things to you.'

A wise man once said the fear of the Lord is awareness of the consequences of disobedience. God's laws are based on the very nature of creation. When we obey, they really work! He gave Adam and Eve one law which they broke. They had to be exiled from paradise so they would not eat of the tree of life and pollute heaven with their foolish and misguided knowledge of what's good and what's evil. He then gave His people Ten Commandments which if they obeyed they would find life. But they didn't keep them either, so He added over 600 more laws, some of which which didn't give life. The law convinced them like a tutor that they could never be good enough to deserve a heavenly reward (Read Ezekiel 20).

Jesus is the second Adam. He came to do what Adam didn't: live a sinless life. Hence He's the perfect Lamb of God who takes away our sins. He alone can reconcile us to God and atone for our iniquity. He gave us the two greatest laws based on one word: "Love". It alone sums up the whole law of life.

I explain the New Testament normative laws of love in my Scriptural Discipleship book *PRECIOUS PEARLS*. It lays this all out in a workbook format that makes it easy to help people understand why it's in their own best interest to learn how to love in all its manifold manifestations as they follow only Jesus. When used as a small group workbook, *PRECIOUS PEARLS* makes it easy to train disciples. Over 95% of the people who took a course using this book became devout Christians, even if they started as agnostics or atheists.

Some may wonder why God says He afflicted His people. He's simply saying they are reaping what they sow. Dung doesn't just happen, it's predictable karma manifesting in this life. When we sin, we fall short of living gloriously. When we commit iniquity (willful evil) we wound others and ourselves. Both sins and iniquities are emotionally harmful to us and usually others.

When I asked a friend who's a Russian holistic doctor what percent of her patient's diseases were rooted in emotional pain she shocked me. She said 100 percent! Even many western medical doctors now admit that over *90% of disease is based on what they call the mind/body connection.* Anxiety is inflammation of the soul and it's the core cause of depression. It's like pain to the body warning us that something is wrong. Stinking thinking can really mess us up.

There's an adage in medicine that the physician sets the bone but God heals the break. The same is true for our hidden buried inner pain and torment.

Only God can heal us. The good news is that He promises to heal ALL our dis-eases (Psalm 103:3).

Jeremiah 30:16-17: *'Therefore all who devour you will be devoured; and all your adversaries, every one of them, will go into captivity; and those who plunder you will be for plunder, and all who prey upon you I will give for prey. 'For I will restore you to health and I will heal you of your wounds,' declares the LORD. 'Because they have called you an outcast, saying: "It is Zion; no one cares for her.' "*

Here's more great news: *we need never seek revenge*. This too is for our own good. Imagine if every false accusation against us is a stone and you've gathered them all up over your whole life and drag them everywhere you go. Stupid, right? But we can do that emotionally. Remember: unforgiveness is like drinking deadly poison and hoping someone else gets sick. Vengeance is the Lord's. So is restoration. When God cures it's because He cares.

Remember: Jesus' earthly ministry was 40% healing and deliverance and just 60% talking. What if churches were like that!

In his book *Seven Reasons Why Churches Rise and Fall*, my friend Bill Gothard says "God condemns pastors who fail to heal." He quotes Ezekiel 34:4,10: *"The diseased you have not strengthened, nor have you healed those who were sick, nor have you bound up the the broken..... Thus says the Lord God, 'Behold, I am against the shepherds, and I will require my flock at their hand; I will cause them to cease feeding the flock."* Gothard then poignantly asks, "Pastor, are you shepherding God's flock or just preaching at them?" He maintains that mental, physical and emotional healing were essential to the first century church and must be a part of churches today (page 28).

Jesus didn't heal and deliver people as a first century PR stunt. He healed because God is all powerful Love. That's why healing and deliverance are for today and every era. They demonstrate God's unfailing love and omnipotent power over ALL evil and dis-ease.

Want more good news: When Jesus bequeathed the Holy Spirit to any who would follow Him, the Spirit didn't come empty handed. *God has given gifted healers to His Church (I Corinthians 12:9) so we can be His earthly hands and feet and facilitate the healing that we all so desperately need.*

Now it really gets good. Look at the awesome catalog of promises God made to us once we receive our healing: Verses 30:18:-24.

(1) "Thus says the LORD, `Behold, I will restore the fortunes of the tents of Jacob and have compassion on his dwelling places." He restores fortunes that were stolen from us; He cares that where we live is safe and secure.

(2) "And the city will be rebuilt on its ruin." That's great news considering the blight and decay in most inner cities.

(3) "And the palace will stand on its rightful place." Palace of government? The wealthy? Probably both.

(4) "From them will proceed thanksgiving and the voice of those who celebrate." Just as He helped rebuild the broken down walls and ravaged cities of old, and put the realm of leadership in its rightful place among the people, He will do the same for His people today. Thanksgiving will become thank-living; joyous celebrations of the God who so loves us will be heard everywhere, and God Himself will occupy the praises of His people. He will dwell both within and among us.

(5) "And I will multiply them and they will not be diminished; I will also honor them and they will not be insignificant." Most Churches that embraced my Transformational Healing Seminars doubled in less than a year! I knew that healing did wonderful things for individuals but I couldn't understand why churches

exploded in growth. When I revisited Jeremiah 30 it all made sense. Healing the broken caused God's people to radiate love and joy. They left our seminars looking five years younger and happier than they'd even been. Friends and neighbors noticed and asked what happened. When they shared that they had received such healing at their church they couldn't wait to attend. They wanted the same blessings for themselves.

(6) "Their children also will be as formerly." Remember when kids didn't have to fear violence and kidnapping?

(7) "And their congregation shall be established before Me; and I will punish all their oppressors." Even their children will respond and become childlike in the best possible ways. Church was the center of their life and community and God dealt with the mockers and anti-christian bigots.

(8) "'Their leader shall be one of them, and their ruler shall come forth from their midst; and I will bring him near and he shall approach Me; for who would dare to risk his life to approach Me?" declares the LORD. Godly leaders will arise from we the people, not the corrupt evil elite.

(9) "You shall be My people, and I will be your God." When the wicked rule, people hide. When truly righteous people govern, the people rejoice. God's people are called to rule in life. Christians comprise about 60% of Americans. If they vote and support righteous candidates they will easily control every election from dog catcher to school board to President. We can again become One

Nation under God. ***Sadly, as of this writing, 25 million Christians are not even registered to vote.*** Pastors: please advocate for righteousness. Dare to get politically involved. If you do it right you won't lose your tax exemption!

In the late 1970's the head of National Right to Life sent me all over the USA to speak to groups of evangelical pastors. At first they questioned why I was advocating that they get involved in politics instead of 'staying in my lane' and preaching the gospel. I showed them from scripture that "God knew us before we were in our mother's womb." He also "hates the death of the innocent" and we are called to protect them. Many accepted that call and shared about abortion with their congregations. Evangelicals swept into the Republican Party and helped get Ronald Reagan elected. My young son saw this and went into politics. He helped carry Ohio in the 2016 election for Donald J Trump and ended up working for him when he was president.

Truly, our example in embracing the whole counsel of God can change nations and expand the spread of the Kingdom Gospel to the entire world!

(10) "Behold, the tempest of the LORD! Wrath has gone forth, a sweeping tempest; it will burst on the head of the wicked. The fierce anger of the LORD will not turn back until He has performed and accomplished the full intent of His heart."

I believe we will see the total unmasking of satanic evil amongst the elite very soon. It's already starting. The era of what I call Presstitues will run its course and corrupt media will be exposed. The Lord's vengeance will be swift and sure. ***God promised this, and He always keeps His promises.***

Finally: Jeremiah 30:24 says "In the latter days you will understand this." I ask God 'Why' quite often. *Why is this healing of wounds so important? Why is it necessary in the latter days? His answer blew my mind!*

He said 'Where sin abounds, pain abounds. There's no such thing as a sin that doesn't hurt anyone. Sin at the very least harms the sinner.'

In the latter days, Satan will pull out the stops and sin will be accepted and destroy countless millions of lives." We see how sin has been sanctioned by society so drug addiction, divorce, suicide, sex trafficking, Satanic Ritual Abuse and violent crimes are ubiquitous. He continued to speak to me:

'Healing broken hearts will be as essential in the 21st Century as healing broken bodies was in the First Century.'

God's promises in Jeremiah 30 reveal His Kingdom Culture, the great good news He desires for us all. They also show us what must happen for that to prevail. There is no medicine or recovery that will heal and restore us. Only God Himself can do that, working through the gifted healers He gave to His Church and every true Christ Follower. ***As that transpires, our prayers for His Kingdom to come on earth as it is in Heaven will finally be answered.*** His Kingdom reign will spread across the globe like a Kingdom Tsunami of love, healing and the bliss of obedience to His laws of Love. Satan will be bound for 1,000 years and every living person ***will be able to see and respond to the righteous reign of God's benevolent New World Order.***

Romans 15 forms a perfect Benediction for the ultimate end time blessing: ***"Now may the God who gives perseverance and encouragement grant you to be of the same mind with one another according to Christ Jesus, so that with one accord you may with one voice glorify the God and Father of our Lord Jesus Christ. Therefore, accept one another, just as Christ also accepted us to the glory of God. For I say that Christ has become a servant to the circumcision on behalf of the truth of God to confirm the promises given to the fathers, and for the Gentiles to glorify God for His mercy; as it is written, 'Therefore I will give praise to You among the Gentiles, and I will sing to Your name.' He says, 'Rejoice, O Gentiles, with His people.' And 'Praise the Lord all you Gentiles, and let all the peoples praise Him.'***

Isaiah says, 'There shall come the root of Jesse, and He who arises to rule over the Gentiles, In Him shall the Gentiles hope.' Now may the God of hope fill you with all joy and peace in believing, so that you will abound in hope by the power of the Holy Spirit."

THAT hope will never disappoint us.

CHAPTER SIXTEEN

KINGDOM FUNDAMENTALS

"The LORD founded the earth by wisdom, He established the heavens by understanding. By His knowledge the ocean depths were burst open, and the clouds drip with dew. My son, see that they do not escape from your sight; Comply with sound wisdom and discretion, And they will be life to your soul And adornment to your neck. Then you will walk in your way securely, And your foot will not stumble. When you lie down, you will not be afraid; When you lie down, your sleep will be sweet. Do not be afraid of sudden danger, Nor of trouble from the wicked when it comes; For the LORD will be your confidence, And will keep your foot from being caught." - Proverbs 3:19-26

FOR THERE TO BE A NEO REFORMATION OF RIGHTEOUSNESS, a mere critique of what's wrong can't accomplish that. We must embrace true scriptural fundamentals. Let's examine what the first Fundamentalists decided and take the next steps further towards the biblical Fundamental Keys the true Church must embrace and embody today.

In the late 19th and early 20th century John Darby, Dwight Moody, B.B. Warfied, Billy Sunday and other Christian leaders saw scriptural morality eroded by pseudo scientific modernism. They were concerned that even biblical theology was also undermined by the 'Higher Criticism' method of interpretation. The book Evidence That Demands a Verdict shows that there is 4,000 times more more proof for the veracity of the Bible than any other historical documents. If we discredit it, nothing else in history can be accurate either.

To express their concerns, a wealthy donor commissioned a twelve volume set that explained the tenants of scripture, then sent 300,000 copies to Christian leaders. These are their conclusions of the Bible's core teaching based on five fundamentals:

1) The whole Bible is literally true and contains no errors; it's meant to be obeyed.

2) Jesus was born to the virgin Mary who conceived him by the Holy Spirit, so He is the fully human and fully divine Son of the Living God.

3) Since Jesus committed no sins, His substitutionary atonement guaranteed that when He died on the cross for the sins of mankind, all can obtain salvation through God's grace and their faith.

4) Jesus physically rose from the dead three days later and sits at our Heavenly Father's right hand.

5) Jesus performed genuine miracles and will return to earth again before the millennium.

These teachings were important in their day. But I should note that most fundamentalists are dispensationalists who believe in a pretribulation rapture. As I said, except for a shallow definition of faith as intellectual assent to doctrine, and the belief in that miracles and healing are not for today, and that we should escape tribulation rather than enter the Kingdom through it, I have no other issues with these fundamentals.

My real issue is that they aren't the fundamental priorities of the Kingdom Gospel that Jesus taught.

Here's Jesus' Fundamentals

1) All God's commands are summed up the mandate to love God with our whole being and all others and our self as Jesus loves us.

2) All Jesus' followers will make disciples of Him not just decisions for Him. How? By teaching them to obey all He commanded.

3) Pastors and missionaries will train the church to do this and to build one another up in love.

4) Since the Kingdom of God is both Internal and Eternal, through being reborn by the same Spirit that raised Jesus from the dead, we share His power to obey Him and even do the works He did and greater.

5) Knowing this, we can become truly Christlike and joint heirs with Him in our Heavenly Father's Kingdom so we can reign in life.

6) By seeking first His Kingdom and righteousness, we receive the abundant life He came to give us. Life on earth becomes more heavenly as we make disciples and teach others the bliss of obedience.

DISCUSSION QUESTIONS

1. How would these Fundamentals change the Church and the world?

____

____

____

____

____

2. What would you have to change for this to become your way,truth and life?

____

____

____

____

____

3. How would your life become better and more abundant by doing this?

____

____

____

____

____

ADDENDUM: ESSENTIAL KINGDOM PASSAGES

KEY KINGDOM VERSES FROM THE NASB TRANSLATION

Daniel 2:37 "You, O king, are the king of kings, to whom the God of heaven has given the kingdom, the power, the strength and the glory;"

Daniel 2:44 "In the days of those kings the God of heaven will set up a kingdom which will never be destroyed, and that kingdom will not be left for another people; it will crush and put an end to all these kingdoms, but it will itself endure forever."

Matthew 12:28 "But if I cast out demons by the Spirit of God, then the kingdom of God has come upon you."

Matthew 19:24 "Again I say to you, it is easier for a camel to go through the eye of a needle, than for a rich man to enter the kingdom of God."

Matthew 21:43 "Therefore I say to you, the kingdom of God will be taken away from you and given to a people, producing the fruit of it."

Mark 1:15 "The time is fulfilled, and the kingdom of God is at hand; repent and believe in the gospel."

Mark 4:11 And He was saying to them, 'To you has been given the mystery of the kingdom of God, but those who are outside get everything in parables.'"

Mark 4:26 And He was saying, "The kingdom of God is like a man who casts seed upon the soil;" ...

Mark 4:30 And He said, "How shall we picture the kingdom of God, or by what parable shall we present it?"

Mark 9:1 And Jesus was saying to them, "Truly I say to you, there are some of those who are standing here who will not taste death until they see the kingdom of God after it has come with power."

Mark 9:47 "If your eye causes you to stumble, throw it out; it is better for you to enter the kingdom of God with one eye, than, having two eyes, to be cast into hell."

Mark 10:14-15 But when Jesus saw this, He was indignant and said to them, "Permit the children to come to Me; do not hinder them; for the kingdom of God belongs to such as these. Truly I say to you, whoever does not receive the

kingdom of God like a child will not enter it at all."
Mark 10:24-5 The disciples were amazed at His words. But Jesus answered again and said to them, "Children, how hard it is to enter the kingdom of God! It is easier for a camel to go through the eye of a needle than for a rich man to enter the kingdom of God."

Mark 12:34 When Jesus saw that he had answered intelligently, He said to him, "You are not far from the kingdom of God." After that, no one would venture to ask Him any more questions.

Mark 14:25 "Truly I say to you, I will never again drink of the fruit of the vine until that day when I drink it new in the kingdom of God."

Luke 4: 43 But He said to them, "I must preach the kingdom of God to the other cities also, for I was sent for this purpose."

Luke 6:20 And turning His gaze toward His disciples, He began to say, "Blessed are you who are poor, for yours is the kingdom of God."

Luke 7:28 "I say to you, among those born of women there is no one greater than John; yet he who is least in the kingdom of God is greater than he."

Luke 8:1 Soon afterwards , He began going around from one city and village to another, proclaiming and preaching

the kingdom of God. The twelve were with Him.
Luke 8:10 And He said, "To you it has been granted to know the mysteries of the kingdom of God, but to the rest it is in parables, so that seeing they may not see, and hearing they may not understand."

Luke 9:2 And He sent them out to proclaim the kingdom of God and to perform healing.

Luke 9:11 But the crowds were aware of this and followed Him; and welcoming them, He began speaking to them about the kingdom of God and curing those who had need of healing.
Luke 9:60 But He said to him, "Allow the dead to bury their own dead; but as for you, go and proclaim everywhere the kingdom of God."

Luke 9:62 But Jesus said to him, "No one, after putting his hand to the plow and looking back, is fit for the kingdom of God."

Luke 10:9 And heal those in it who are sick, and say to them, 'The kingdom of God has come near to you.'"

Luke 10:11 "Even the dust of your city which clings to our feet we wipe off in protest against you; yet be sure of this, that the kingdom of God has come near."

Luke 13:18 So He was saying, "What is the kingdom of God like, and to what shall I compare it?"

Luke 13:28 "In that place there will be weeping and gnashing of teeth when you see Abraham and Isaac and Jacob and all the prophets in the kingdom of God, but yourselves being thrown out."

Luke 13:29 "And they will come from east and west and from north and south, and will recline at the table in the kingdom of God."

Luke 14:15 When one of those who were reclining at the table with Him heard this, he said to Him, "Blessed is everyone who will eat bread in the kingdom of God!"

Luke 16:16 "The Law and the Prophets were proclaimed until John; since that time the gospel of the kingdom of God has been preached, and everyone is forcing his way into it."

Luke 17:20-21 Now having been questioned by the Pharisees as to when the kingdom of God was coming, He answered them and said, "The kingdom of God is not coming with signs to be observed; Nor will they say, 'Look, here it is!' or, 'There it is!' For behold, the kingdom of God is in your midst."

Luke 18:24 And Jesus looked at him and said, "How hard it is for those who are wealthy to enter the kingdom of God!"

Luke 18:29 And He said to them, "Truly I say to you, there is no one who has left house or wife or brothers or parents or children, for the sake of the kingdom of God, Concerning the rapture: While they were listening to these things, Jesus went on to tell a parable, because He was near Jerusalem, and they supposed that the kingdom of God was going to appear immediately. Many think that today? I suggest you read all of Luke 21 carefully, noting the sequence of events. It is the best passage for understanding who will escape tribulation and how they will escape it.

Luke 21:31 "So you also, when you see these things happening, recognize that the kingdom of God is near."

Luke 22:16 "For I say to you, I shall never again eat it until it is fulfilled in the kingdom of God."

John 3:3 Jesus answered and said to him, "Truly, truly, I say to you, unless one is born again he cannot see the kingdom of God."

John 3:5 Jesus answered, "Truly, truly, I say to you, unless one is born of water and the Spirit he cannot enter into the kingdom of God."

Acts 1:3 To these He (Jesus) also presented Himself alive after His suffering, by many convincing proofs, appearing to them over a period of forty days and speaking of the things concerning the kingdom of God.

Acts 8:12 But when they believed Philip preaching the good news about the kingdom of God and the name of Jesus Christ, they were being baptized, men and women alike. Acts 14:22 ... strengthening the souls of the disciples, encouraging them to continue in the faith, and saying, "Through many tribulations we must enter the kingdom of God." Acts 19:8 And he entered the synagogue and continued speaking out boldly for three months, reasoning and persuading them about the kingdom of God.

Acts 28:23 When they had set a day for Paul, they came to him at his lodging in large numbers; and he was explaining to them by solemnly testifying about the kingdom of God and trying to persuade them concerning Jesus, from both the Law of Moses and from the Prophets, from morning until evening.

Acts 28:31 ... preaching the kingdom of God and teaching concerning the Lord Jesus Christ with all openness, unhindered.

Romans 14: 11 For the kingdom of God is not eating and drinking, but righteousness and peace and joy in the Holy Spirit..

I Corinthians 4:20 For the kingdom of God does not consist in words but in power.

1 Corinthians 6:9-10 Or do you not know that the

unrighteous will not inherit the kingdom of God? Do not be deceived; neither fornicators, nor idolaters, nor adulterers, nor effeminate, nor homosexuals, nor thieves, nor the covetous, nor drunkards, nor revilers, nor swindlers, will inherit the kingdom of God."

1 Corinthians 15:50 "Now I say this, brethren, that flesh and blood cannot inherit the kingdom of God; nor does the perishable inherit the imperishable."

Galatians 5:21 NAS ... Envying, drunkenness, carousing, and things like these, of which I forewarn you, just as I have forewarned you, that those who practice such things will not inherit the kingdom of God.

Ephesians 5:5 For this you know with certainty, that no immoral or impure person or covetous man, who is an idolater, has an inheritance in the kingdom of Christ and God.

1 Thessalonians 2:12..so that you would walk in a manner worthy of the God who calls you into His own kingdom and glory.
2 Thessalonians 1:5 This is a plain indication of God's righteous judgment so that you will be considered worthy of the kingdom of God, for which indeed you are suffering.

2 Timothy 4:1 I solemnly charge you in the presence of God and of Christ Jesus, who is to judge the living and the dead, and by His appearing and His kingdom:

Hebrews 1:8 But of the Son He says, "Your throne O God, is forever and ever, and the righteous scepter is the scepter of his kingdom."

James 2:5 "Listen, my beloved brethren: did not God choose the poor of this world to be rich in faith and heirs of the kingdom which He promised to those who love Him?"

Revelation 1:9 "I, John, your brother and fellow partaker in the tribulation and kingdom and perseverance which are in Jesus, was on the island called Patmos because of the word of God and the testimony of Jesus."

Revelation 12:10 "Then I heard a loud voice in heaven, saying, 'Now the salvation, and the power, and the kingdom of our God and the authority of His Christ have come, for the accuser of our brethren has been thrown down, he who accuses them before our God day and night.'"

Revelation 17:17 "For God has put it in their hearts to execute His purpose by having a common purpose, and by giving their kingdom to the beast, until the words of God will be fulfilled.

Want more? A simple web search will show you every verse in the Bible on God's Heavenly Kingdom.

Last but certainly not least: The King of king's kids are also Priests:

> *I Peter 2:9-12, 15_ "But you are A CHOSEN PEOPLE, A royal PRIESTHOOD, A HOLY NATION, A PEOPLE FOR God's own possession, so that you may proclaim the excellencies of Him who has called you out of darkness into His marvelous light; for you once were NOT A PEOPLE, but now you are THE PEOPLE OF God; you had NOT RECEIVED MERCY, but now you have RECEIVED MERCY (lovingkindness). Dear friends, I urge you as strangers and exiles to abstain from sinful desires that wage war against the soul. Keep your behavior excellent among the Gentiles, so that in the thing in which they slander you as evildoers, they may, because of your good deeds, as they observe them, glorify God on the day of visitation. For such is the will of God, that by doing right you silence the ignorance of foolish people."*

CONCLUSION

I'VE SHARED WITH YOU SOME exciting and beautiful things along with some fearsome and controversial things. Don't take my word for any of it; only trust God's. I suggest you research every word for Hell in the King James Bible and compare the notes in the NASB Bible's accurate literal translation. You can easily do this online.

A major reason Jesus didn't warn sinners about Hell is because His gospel of the Kingdom begins here and now, not there and then. Another reason? Our heavenly Father is a just, loving and righteous God who doesn't want anyone to perish, especially those who aren't evil. Why would He subject them to eternal torment if they never had an opportunity to know Him? I'm sure that Hell is for Satan, his demons, and those who choose to obey them. The literal Bible and centuries of Near Death Experiences confirm this.

But the best part of the Kingdom gospel for this life is the 7,500 promises in the Bible. Only 750 are in the New Testament. The entire inspired Bible is so comprehensive that His followers can apply it to every aspect of life from health, wealth and healing to relationships, success, receiving God's help and favor and everything in between. To those who reject the relevance of the Old Testament I'd ask this: do you only want to acquire the 10% of God's promises found in the New? As a wise dentist once said, 'Only floss the teeth you want to keep!"

Following leading of Jesus can guide us all to an abundant life in every possible sense of the word. That's why He commanded the apostles to make disciples of all, not just decisions for Him. He's not begging anyone to accept His awesome great news. When He lived on earth He even offered it to the ultra religious leaders knowing some would reject and kill Him for doing so.

Those who love Jesus obey and thus abide in Him. Many scriptures confirm this. (Study John's epistles.) Therefore God will grant their every request (John 15). But God isn't doing this as a theological quid pro quo. He did it so His followers will receive the fullest Joy, Love, Righteousness, Shalom, and other delectable fruits of the Holy Spirit that make our life meaningful, exciting and just plain glorious. God's awesome plan for you will prosper you not harm you and give you eternal hope and a divine future (Jeremiah 29:11-12). He absolutely delights in the prosperity of all His *servants* (Psalm 37).

As soon as I finally embraced God's Kingdom promises and obeyed Him with my whole heart, my life became so good I'll never retire! My Boss truly is my BFF (Best Friend Forever). He can use me anyway He wants to share His complete Kingdom gospel with the world. Doors are opening for that and I can't wait to walk through them!

Even agnostics and atheists who don't believe in heaven or hell fear death and its torment (Hebrews 2:14-15). But Jesus can free us from all such fears. I'm beyond eager to help all people find true freedom and bliss, aren't you? What a wonder filled world it will be! You too can help loved ones, family, friends, neighbors and others who also want to become joint heirs in His Heavenly Kingdom. Think about this: we can all do the works Jesus did and greater. We are truly the Body of Christ: His physical Presence on earth today.

After helping over 40 impossible cases heal and almost 20 avoid suicide I can tell you that there's no greater joy than seeing God work through you. It's the best way to live; the only way to live abundantly. And it's well worth dying for. When you're truly reborn, you know beyond all doubt that Jesus is alive, heaven is real, and our eternal retirement benefits are even greater than what the Kingdom Gospel has for us in this life.

The story of Steven, one of the first deacons (servants) and the very the first Christian martyr comes to mind. I recently shared it with a bank teller named Steven who didn't know his name is biblical. I told him how the scriptural Steven looked up into Jesus' eyes and smiled as they stoned him to death (Acts 6-8). He was surprised to learn that and how this impacted the religious scholar Saul of Tarsus who encouraged Steven's stoning. When he saw how he joyfully dies, Saul knew Heaven is real and Jesus was the one who could get him there. Saul surrendered to Jesus and was transformed into the Apostle Paul, who wrote about 60% of the New Testament. Near the end of his life, Paul shared that he was blessed and honored to partake in Christ's sufferings until he too was martyred for sharing Jesus' gospel along with the very Gentiles he formerly hated! But I must remind you of one essential caveat.

Jesus will not return until the Gospel of the Kingdom is shared in every nation.

It's hardly proclaimed in the United States. Our work is cut out for us. Jesus has a message and a mission for us all. He wants every true Christian to enlist in His army. Global translators must see that the complete Kingdom Gospel is available in every language. (This is now easily accomplished through AI.) Those who live in each nation must share it and disciple those who embrace it. Only then can it reach every nation and person in the world. Only then can heaven on earth begin. Only then will our heavenly Father(who wills that none should perish) be satisfied that everything necessary has been completed. Then His chosen people can rule on earth for 1,000 years. Read Isaiah chapter 2: this is possibly unfolding today! Jesus confirmed all this in His Olivet discourse in the synoptic gospels.

Also read Luke 21 carefully. It tells you how you can avoid tribulation! And Revelations promises that those who endure till the end will be saved.

Note: I've created the following items to help you TRAIN PEOPLE AND CHURCHES TO HEAL AND MAKE DISCIPLES.

Pastors have said, "No matter what your denomination is, Ken's discipleship workbook *PRECIOUS PEARLS* offers you the best tool to equip your church to make disciples."

"Some of the greatest men in the world mentored me: Napoleon Hill, Bill Bright, Norman Vincent Peale, Zig Ziglar, and now Ken Unger. He writes so impact-fully his book will transform your life." - John Carr, Founder, Charitable Giving Foundation.

His end time healing workbook *PEACE WITHOUT PROZAC* will train your Church to heal inner wounds in the latter days as God promised in Jeremiah 30.

"We all need healing. Here is your effortless exit to healing bliss." - Mark Victor Hansen, Founder, Chicken Soup for the Soul.

TRANSFORMATIONAL HEALING trains people to heal the core personal pain that causes addictions. Churches and prisons use these three books to heal and equip God's people for discipleship, healing and conquering addiction.

"We always knew that emotional pain causes addiction. Ken showed us how to heal it." - Dr. Karl Benzio, Medical Director for Honey Lake Clinic and the American Association of Christian Counselors.

Churches can order bulk copies of Ken's books at a discount as well as audio books, video courses and other tools at www.SoulDr.com. It contains over 40 years of testimonies and Letters of Reference from counseling and church professionals as well as lay people. It also has info on you can become a Certified Transformational Counselor, Clergy, Chaplain and Spiritual Mentors.

Sign up for your free monthly newsletter today at www.SoulDr.com

ABOUT THE AUTHOR

Ken Unger is "America's Soul Doctor," a true spiritual healer. A former pastor, spiritual psychotherapist, and former professor of counseling, he knows how to heal your broken places.

He has been leading retreats on personal growth and healing all across the United States for over 40 years. Now his solid scriptural wisdom is available to you.

Don't treat your symptoms, heal your pain. When you heal your pain you no longer need aspirin in whatever form you take it. Don't just care for your soul, cure it! Learn more at www.SoulDr.com.

www.ingramcontent.com/pod-product-compliance
Lightning Source LLC
LaVergne TN
LVHW010644110826
845149LV00014B/2952

* 9 7 8 1 9 6 1 0 0 3 0 5 7 *